Applied Artificial Intelligence

ESSENTIALS EDITION

Kimberly Seefeld, EdD

Table of contents

Applied Artificial Intelligence

ESSENTIALS EDITION

By Kimberly Seefeld, EdD

Published under **DataJoyAI** imprint

Edition: First Edition
ISBN: 978-1-969233-25-8

Chapter 1

AI-Driven Business Automation

1.1 Introduction

Think about your morning routine. You might ask Siri to set a reminder, check your bank app for account updates, or receive a personalized news feed on your phone. Behind each of these simple interactions, artificial intelligence is working to automate processes that used to require human effort.

This is the reality of AI-driven business automation – technology that can think, learn, and make decisions to handle tasks that once needed human intelligence. Unlike the simple automation of the past, today's AI systems can understand natural language, recognize patterns, and adapt to new situations.

The numbers tell an impressive story. Companies using AI automation report reducing processing time by up to 80% while improving accuracy to over 95% [1]. More importantly, these businesses aren't just doing things faster – they're discovering entirely new ways to serve customers and create value.

Consider Netflix's recommendation system. It doesn't just suggest random movies; it learns your preferences, analyzes viewing patterns, and predicts what you'll enjoy watching next. This AI automation has become so effective that 80% of what people watch on Netflix comes from these personalized recommendations [2].

But what makes AI automation different from the automation we've had for decades? How do you know which business processes are ready for AI? And what tools are making this transformation possible? This chapter will answer these fundamental questions and give you the foundation to understand AI automation in business.

1.2 Understanding Business Process Automation

1.2.1 What is Business Process Automation?

Business process automation means using technology to handle tasks that people used to do manually. Think of it as teaching computers to do routine work so humans can focus on more creative and strategic activities.

Traditional automation has been around for decades. Assembly lines in factories, automatic bill payments, and email autoreplies are all examples of basic automation. These systems follow simple rules: "If this happens, then do that." They work well for predictable, repetitive tasks but struggle when situations change or unexpected problems arise.

AI automation takes this concept much further. Instead of just following rules, AI systems can learn from experience, understand context, and make intelligent decisions. They can handle messy, real-world situations that would confuse traditional automation systems.

1.2.2 Key Capabilities of AI Automation

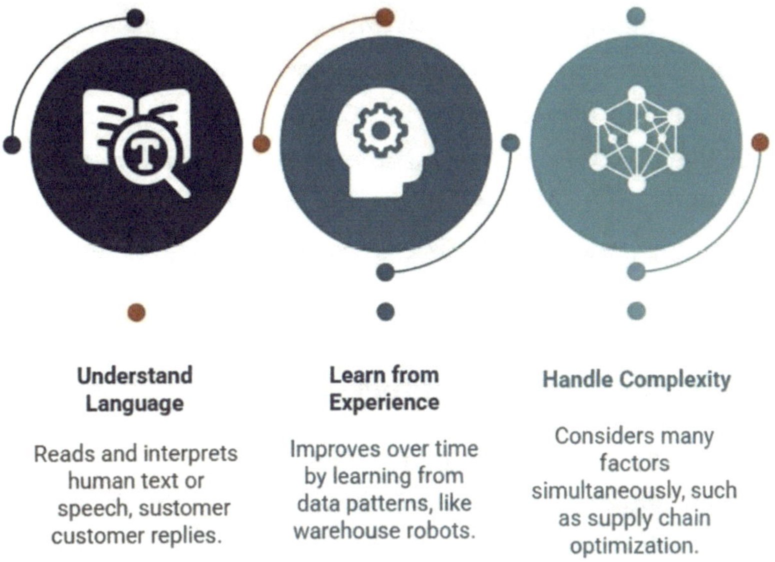

Artificial intelligence has several key capabilities that make it powerful in real-world applications. Understanding natural language means that AI can read and interpret human communication. For example, a customer service AI can understand a statement like, "My order is late and I'm frustrated," and respond appropriately, addressing the customer's concerns. Learning from experience allows AI systems to improve over time by analyzing patterns in the data they encounter. A practical example of this is Amazon's warehouse robots, which enhance efficiency by learning from millions of package movements. Finally, handling complexity refers to AI's ability to consider multiple factors simultaneously when making decisions. For instance, supply chain AI can analyze weather conditions, supplier availability, costs, and consumer demand all at once to optimize operations.

1.2.3 Real-World Examples

AI automation is transforming many common business processes in significant ways. In smart customer service, traditional systems route calls based on menu selections, but AI-enhanced systems can analyze voice emotion, understand customer questions, and connect callers to the right solution. For example, Bank of America's virtual assistant Erica handles over 1 billion customer requests per year [3]. In intelligent document processing, employees traditionally type invoice information manually into computer systems. With AI, documents are read automatically, key information is extracted, and databases are updated without human intervention. JPMorgan Chase now analyzes legal documents in seconds—work that previously required 360,000 lawyer hours annually [4]. Finally, in predictive maintenance, organizations used to wait for equipment to break down before fixing it. AI systems can now predict failures by analyzing sensor data and usage patterns, reducing unexpected downtime by up to 50% in manufacturing [5].

1.2.4 The Automation Maturity Journey

Organizations typically progress through three distinct levels as they adopt more sophisticated automation. Level 1, Basic Task Automation, involves simple, rule-based processes such as automatic email responses or scheduled reports. These systems handle routine work but still require human intervention for exceptions. Level 2, Process Orchestration, occurs when multiple automated tasks work together. For example, when you order online, systems can automatically verify payment, update inventory, generate shipping labels, and send confirmations without manual effort. Level 3, Intelligent Optimization, is where AI systems not only execute processes but continuously improve them. They can identify bottlenecks, predict problems, and optimize performance in real time, adapting to new information as it becomes available.

1.3 AI-Driven vs. Traditional Rule-Based Automation

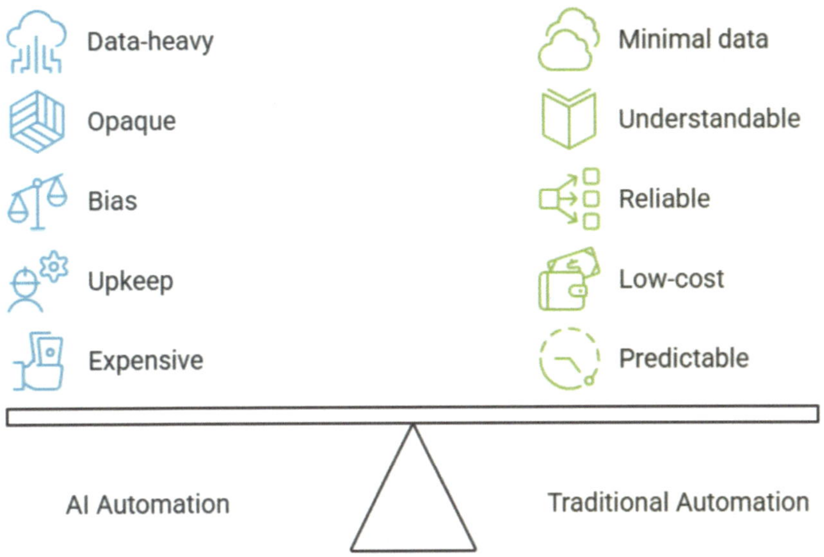

Understanding the difference between traditional and AI automation is crucial for recognizing when each approach works best. The fundamental distinction lies in how they handle unexpected situations and make decisions.

1.3.1 The Core Difference: Flexibility vs. Consistency

The core difference between traditional automation and AI automation lies in flexibility versus consistency. Traditional automation follows a strict script: if the script does not cover a particular situation, the system fails or requires human intervention. It is like following a recipe exactly—if one ingredient is missing, the process comes to a halt. In contrast, AI automation can adapt and make reasonable decisions even in new situations. It behaves like a skilled cook who can substitute ingredients and adjust techniques based on what is available and what will produce the best result.

1.3.2 Comparing Traditional and AI Automation in Business Processes

Email customer service provides a clear example of how traditional automation and AI automation differ. Traditional systems typically scan specific keywords and respond using pre-written templates. They cannot detect customer frustration, remain the same unless manually updated, and often fail or forward unusual situations to human agents. In contrast, AI-powered systems understand the meaning and intent behind messages, provide personalized and contextual responses, adjust their tone based on customer emotions, improve with every interaction, and adapt to new situations without explicit reprogramming.

The COVID-19 pandemic offered a real-world test of automation flexibility. When business conditions changed rapidly, traditional systems struggled and required extensive manual reprogramming to accommodate new payment terms, modified services, and altered processes. AI systems, however, adapted gracefully: customer service chatbots quickly learned to handle pandemic-related questions, and supply chain AI automatically identified alternative suppliers and shipping routes when disruptions occurred [6].

Decision-making approaches also highlight the differences. Traditional automation relies on binary decisions—yes or no based on exact criteria—and fixed rules such as "if credit score is greater than 700, approve loan." The outcomes are predictable, with the same input always producing the same result. AI automation, on the other hand, makes contextual decisions, weighing multiple factors and probabilities. It uses pattern analysis that considers credit score, spending habits, employment history, and broader economic trends, resulting in adaptive outcomes where the same input may produce different outputs depending on the context.

1.3.3 When to Choose Each Approach

Traditional automation is the best choice when a process is highly predictable and rarely changes, when guaranteed, consistent results are required every time, when the rules are simple and well-defined, when cost is a primary concern—since traditional automation is usually cheaper to implement—and when regulatory compliance demands exact, auditable processes. In contrast, AI automation is preferable when a process involves judgment calls or interpretation, when you are working with unstructured data such as emails, documents, or images, when the environment changes frequently, when you want the system to improve over time, or when customer experience and personalization are priorities.

1.3.4 Understanding the Limitations

While AI automation offers impressive capabilities, it is important to understand its limitations. AI systems require large amounts of high-quality data to learn effectively, can be difficult to explain in terms of how decisions are made, may perpetuate biases present in the training data, and need ongoing monitoring and maintenance. Additionally, implementing and maintaining AI can be expensive.

Traditional automation, on the other hand, has several advantages. It is completely predictable and auditable, generally involves lower implementation and maintenance costs, works well with limited data, is easy to understand and troubleshoot, and is highly reliable for compliance-critical processes.

1.4 Categorizing Business Processes for AI Automation

Not every business process benefits from AI automation. Smart organizations use a systematic approach to identify the best opportunities and avoid costly mistakes. This section will help you develop that evaluation framework.

1.4.1 The AI Suitability Framework

The AI Suitability Framework helps organizations determine which processes are good candidates for AI automation by evaluating three key dimensions: data availability, decision complexity, and business impact. Data availability refers to the quantity and quality of data that can be used for training AI. Processes with rich, varied data sources are highly suitable, while those with some structured data are moderately suitable, and processes with limited or poor-quality data are low-suitability candidates. Decision complexity measures how much judgment or pattern recognition is required. Tasks that require sophisticated analysis and interpretation are ideal for AI, whereas simple, rule-based decisions are better suited for traditional automation. Business impact assesses the importance of the process to the organization. High-volume, customer-facing, or cost-critical processes are highly suitable for AI, moderate-impact tasks fall in the middle, and low-impact or low-risk processes are generally poor candidates.

High-suitability processes benefit most from AI capabilities. In customer service and support, AI excels because of natural language interactions, personalization needs, and abundant conversation data. AI systems provide 24/7 availability, consistent quality, and continuous learning from interactions. For example, Spotify's AI can understand a question like, "Why isn't my family plan working?" and provide personalized troubleshooting. In financial processing and analysis, AI handles large data volumes with high accuracy requirements, enabling real-time fraud detection, automated reporting, and predictive insights. Credit card companies, for instance, can analyze transaction patterns instantly, flagging fraudulent activity while allowing legitimate purchases. Supply chain and inventory management is another high-suitability area because it involves multiple variables, prediction requirements, and optimization opportunities. Walmart, for example, predicts product demand by analyzing weather, events, sales history, and social media trends [7].

Medium-suitability processes are partially suitable for AI, often requiring human oversight. In human resources and recruitment, AI can assist with resume screening, candidate matching, and performance pattern analysis, but cultural fit and leadership assessment still require human judgment. The best approach is AI-assisted screening with humans making the final decisions. In marketing and advertising, AI can optimize campaigns, target audiences, and personalize content, while creative strategy and brand messaging remain human-led. Quality control and compliance can benefit from AI in pattern recognition, anomaly detection, and consistency checking, but complex regulation interpretation and ethical considerations necessitate expert human review.

Low-suitability processes are those where AI currently plays a supporting role rather than a primary one. Strategic planning and leadership require human judgment, ethical reasoning, and management of stakeholder relationships; AI can assist through data analysis and scenario modeling. Creative and innovation work demands breakthrough thinking, emotional intelligence, and cultural sensitivity, with AI serving as a research or idea-generation tool. Finally, complex relationship management, including negotiation, conflict resolution, and trust-building, remains human-driven, though AI can provide background research and communication insights to support decision-making.

1.4.2 Implementation Priority Matrix

Table 1.1: Business Impact vs. AI Suitability Matrix

Business Impact	High Suitability	Medium Suitability	Low Suitability
High	Start here: Customer service, Financial processing	Quick wins: Document processing, Basic analytics	Consider later: Internal reporting
Medium	Phase 2: HR screening, Marketing optimization	Evaluate ROI: Quality control, Compliance monitoring	Low priority: Internal communications
Low	Human–AI partnership: Strategic planning support	AI-assisted: Creative tools, Research help	Avoid: Pure relationship work

1.4.3 Risk Factors to Consider

Before implementing AI automation, organizations should carefully evaluate potential risks across technical, business, and ethical dimensions. Technical risks include data quality issues that can lead to poor AI performance, system complexity that makes maintenance difficult, challenges integrating AI with existing systems, and scalability limitations as the business grows. Business risks involve over-reliance on AI for critical decisions, the potential loss of human expertise and institutional knowledge, customer dissatisfaction with impersonal service, and the possibility of a competitive disadvantage if implementation fails. Ethical and legal risks encompass bias in AI decision-making that can affect fairness, privacy concerns related to data collection and use, regulatory compliance challenges, and accountability issues when AI makes mistakes. By understanding these risks upfront, organizations can plan mitigation strategies and ensure AI deployment adds value safely and responsibly.

1.5 AI Tools Transforming Business Operations

The AI automation landscape includes hundreds of tools and platforms. Rather than overwhelming you with options, this section organizes the major categories by business use case and provides a practical framework for understanding what each type of tool does best.

1.5.1 AI Tool Categories by Business Function

1.5.1.1 Customer Interaction Tools

Customer interaction tools manage communications with customers through chat, voice, and email. They are especially useful for businesses with high customer service volumes or 24/7 support needs. Examples include chatbots, which handle FAQs and order status inquiries; voice assistants, which support phone-based customer service and voice ordering; and email AI, which assists with routing and drafting responses. These tools range from low to medium implementation complexity. Case Example: H&M's AI assistant handles 67% of customer inquiries automatically while maintaining high customer satisfaction, allowing human agents to focus on more complex issues.

1.5.1.2 Document and Data Processing Tools

Document and data processing tools read, understand, and extract information from business documents, making them ideal for organizations that process large volumes of invoices, contracts, or forms. Common tools include Document AI for invoice processing and contract analysis, data entry automation for form digitization and data extraction, and intelligent OCR for handling handwritten text or poor-quality scans. Implementation complexity ranges from low to medium. Case Example: Insurance companies use these tools to process claims in hours rather than days by automatically reading documents, assessing damages from photos, and verifying coverage.

1.5.1.3 Analytics and Prediction Tools

Analytics and prediction tools examine data patterns to forecast trends, optimize performance, and guide strategic decisions. Key tools include predictive analytics platforms for demand forecasting and risk assessment, business intelligence software for automated insights and trend detection, and recommendation engines for personalized product or content suggestions. Implementation complexity varies from medium to high. Case Example: Netflix leverages predictive analytics to decide which shows to produce and how to market them, resulting in successful series such as Stranger Things.

1.5.1.4 Process Automation Tools

Process automation tools streamline complex workflows involving multiple systems and decision points. They are best suited for organizations with repetitive, multi-step processes. Tools include AI-enhanced robotic process automation (RPA) for claims processing and account reconciliation, workflow automation platforms for cross-system data flow and approvals, and integration platforms for connecting multiple AI tools. Implementation complexity ranges from medium to high. Case Example: Financial services firms use AI-enhanced RPA to process loan applications, reducing approval times from days to hours while improving accuracy.

1.5.2 Choosing the Right Tool: A Decision Framework

1.5.2.1 Start with Your Business Need

Selecting the right AI tool begins by identifying the problem you want to solve. If the goal is to improve customer service, chatbots, voice AI, and email automation are the primary options, with a simple chatbot for common questions being a practical starting point. For faster document processing, tools such as Document AI, OCR, and data extraction are appropriate, beginning with automating invoice processing. Organizations aiming to make better predictions should consider predictive analytics or business intelligence tools, focusing first on sales forecasting or inventory optimization. Finally, when automating complex workflows, robotic process automation (RPA) or workflow automation platforms can be applied, with initial efforts targeting one specific multi-step process.

1.5.2.2 Consider Implementation Factors

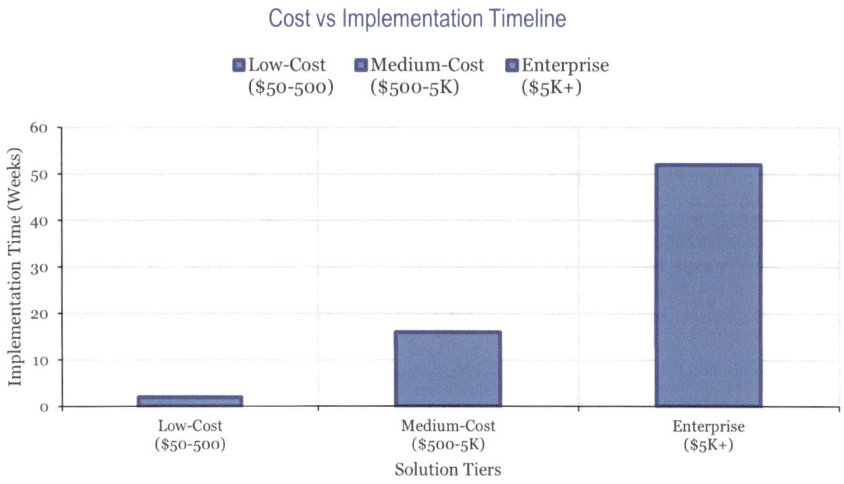

Budget, technical expertise, and time to value are critical in selecting a tool. Low-cost options, including chatbots and basic workflow automation, typically range from $50 to $500 per month. Medium-cost solutions, such as document processing and business intelligence tools, generally fall between $500 and $5,000 per month. High-cost implementations, including custom predictive analytics or enterprise-scale RPA, often exceed $5,000 per month. Technical requirements vary pre-built chatbots and simple workflow tools require minimal expertise, document processing and BI systems demand moderate skill, and custom AI models or complex RPA implementations require significant technical knowledge. Time to value also differs. Quick wins, achievable in one to three months, include chatbots and document processing. Medium-term projects, taking three to six months, include predictive analytics and advanced workflow automation, while long-term initiatives exceeding six months involve enterprise-wide automation and fully customized AI solutions.

By assessing business need alongside budget, technical capability, and expected time to value, organizations can make informed decisions, start small, and scale AI implementations effectively.

1.5.3 Understanding Tool Limitations and Risks

Even the best AI tools have limitations that organizations must understand before implementation. From a technical perspective, AI requires clean, well-organized data to function effectively, can struggle with edge cases or unusual situations, demands ongoing maintenance and updates, and may be difficult to integrate with legacy systems. Business implementation also carries risks, including over-automation that reduces human oversight, employee resistance to new technologies, vendor lock-in with proprietary platforms, and hidden costs associated with training, maintenance, and upgrades. Performance expectations should be realistic: AI tools typically achieve 80 to 95 percent accuracy rather than perfection, and initial performance may be lower until the system has learned from sufficient data. Ultimately, success depends heavily on data quality and quantity, as well as continuous monitoring and adjustment to ensure the tools deliver reliable and actionable results.

1.5.4 Getting Started: A Practical Roadmap

Phase 1: Foundation (Months 1–3) focuses on selecting a high-impact, low-complexity AI tool and starting with a pilot project in a non-critical area. The goal is to build internal capability, learn from the experience, and measure results while gathering user feedback.

Phase 2: Expansion (Months 4–9) involves scaling successful pilots to broader use, adding complementary tools that integrate smoothly, developing internal expertise and best practices, and beginning to address more complex automation opportunities.

Phase 3: Optimization (Months 10+) emphasizes integrating multiple AI tools into comprehensive workflows, leveraging advanced analytics to optimize performance, exploring custom solutions for unique business needs, and sharing learnings to expand automation across other areas of the business.

1.6 Conclusion

This chapter introduced the foundations of AI-driven business automation, highlighting the differences between traditional and AI approaches. Traditional automation relies on fixed rules and excels at predictable tasks, while AI automation can learn, adapt, and manage complex, unstructured situations. Both approaches have value, and choosing between them depends on business needs, risk tolerance, and available resources.

Not all processes are equally suited for AI. The Process Suitability Framework identifies the best candidates: those with rich data, complex decision-making, and significant business impact. High-suitability processes include customer service, financial processing, and supply chain management, whereas strategic planning and creative work remain primarily human-driven.

Successful implementation requires a strategic approach. Start small with high-impact, low-complexity processes to gain experience and demonstrate value. Focus on areas where AI's unique capabilities—learning, adaptation, and pattern recognition—provide clear advantages. Selecting the right tools involves aligning them with specific business functions, integration requirements, costs, and implementation complexity, while remembering that tools alone do not guarantee success.

AI automation offers significant benefits, including efficiency improvements, enhanced accuracy, 24/7 availability, the ability to manage complex decisions, and continuous learning. However, it also has limitations: it requires high-quality data and ongoing maintenance, can be costly, may struggle with edge cases, poses ethical risks, and can reduce human oversight if overused.

Looking ahead, AI is best understood as augmenting human intelligence rather than replacing it. Professionals should complement AI with skills in critical thinking, ethical reasoning, human-centered design, and clear communication. For businesses, thoughtful and gradual implementation of AI automation can deliver competitive advantages, improve efficiency, and enhance human capabilities, while maintaining ethical and strategic oversight.

Chapter 2

AI Assistants and Copilots

2.1 Introduction

Imagine starting your workday by asking an AI assistant to summarize yesterday's meeting notes, draft a follow-up email, and create a project timeline – all while you grab your morning coffee. This isn't science fiction; it's how millions of professionals already work with AI assistants in 2025.

AI assistants and copilots represent a fundamental shift from traditional software tools. Instead of learning complex menus and commands, you can simply describe what you need in plain English. These intelligent partners can write code, create presentations, analyze data, and even help you brainstorm solutions to complex problems.

The impact has been remarkable. Companies using AI assistants report that employees save 2-3 hours per day on routine tasks, while developers using GitHub Copilot complete coding tasks 55% faster. But AI assistants aren't just about speed – they're about augmenting human capabilities rather than replacing them.

This chapter will help you understand how AI assistants work, when to use them effectively, and how to integrate them into professional workflows. We'll explore real-world applications and learn to recognize when human judgment should take precedence over AI recommendations.

2.2 Understanding AI Assistants and Copilots

2.2.1 What Makes AI Assistants Different

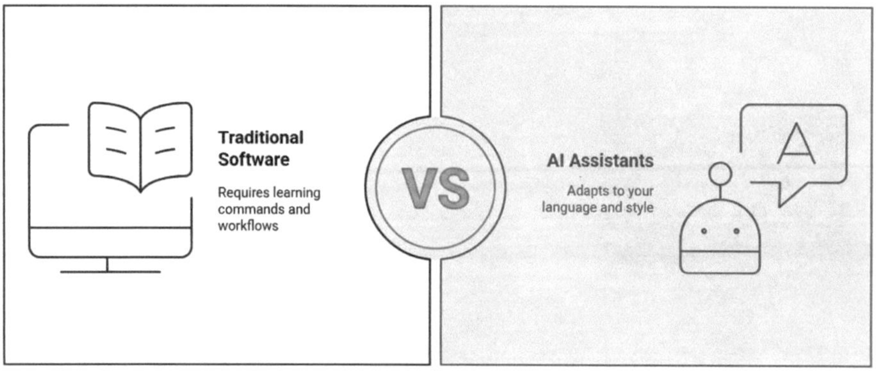

AI assistants represent a new category of software that fundamentally changes how we interact with technology. Traditional software requires you to learn its language – specific commands, menu structures, and workflows. AI assistants flip this relationship: they learn to understand your language and adapt to your working style.

Think of the difference between using a traditional spreadsheet program and asking an AI assistant for help with data analysis. With traditional software, you need to know formulas, functions, and formatting commands. With an AI assistant, you can simply say, "Help me find trends in this sales data and create a chart showing the results."

2.2.2 The Three Types of AI Work Partners

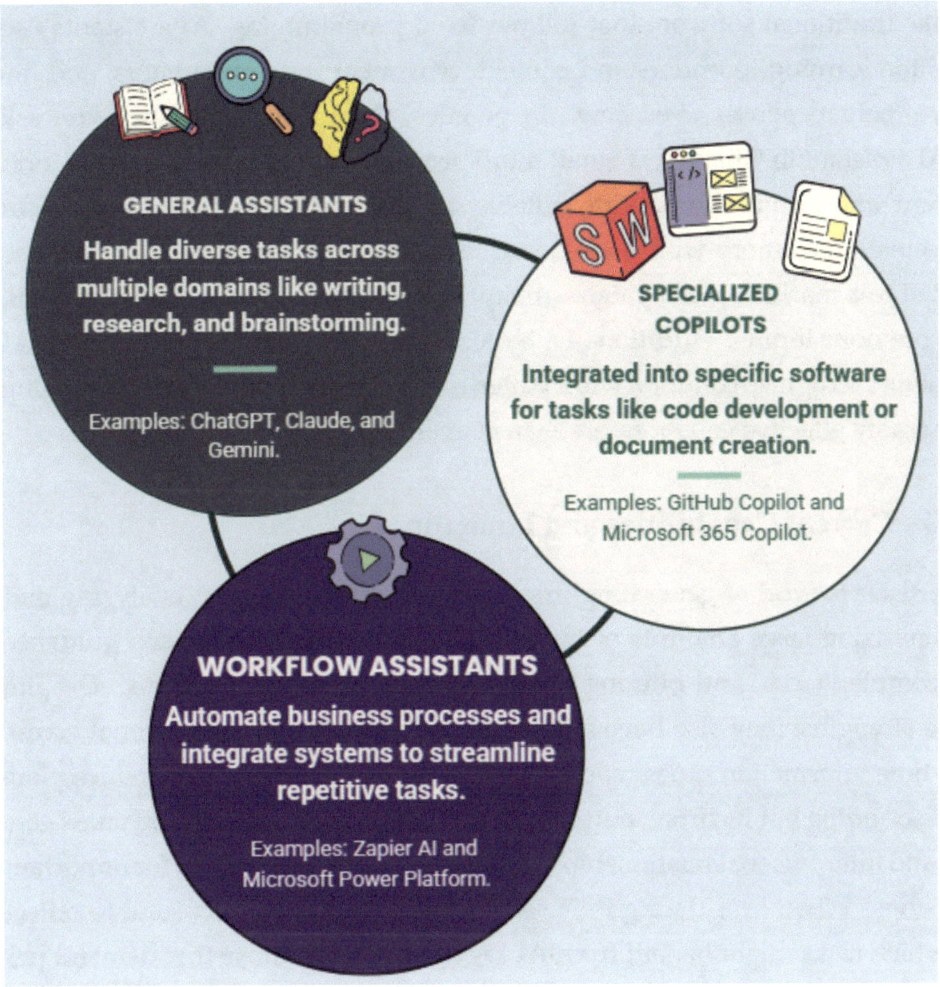

AI work partners can be categorized into three main types, each serving distinct purposes. General assistants, such as ChatGPT, Claude, and Gemini, handle diverse tasks across multiple domains and are best suited for writing, research, and brainstorming. Specialized copilots are integrated into specific software platforms, with examples including GitHub Copilot and Microsoft 365 Copilot, making them ideal for code development or document creation within those environments. Workflow assistants, such as Zapier AI and Microsoft Power Platform, focus on automating business processes and integrating systems to streamline repetitive tasks. A key insight is that AI assistants excel at understanding context and maintaining conversation memory within a session, which allows them to function more like collaborative partners than traditional tools.

2.2.3 How AI Assistants Learn and Adapt

Unlike traditional software that follows fixed programming, AI assistants use machine learning to understand context, remember user preferences, and improve their responses over time. In practice, this means that when you ask an AI assistant to "make this email more professional," it can analyze the tone, content, and purpose to provide suitable suggestions. AI assistants also retain conversation memory within a session, so follow-up questions—such as those related to a marketing campaign—maintain awareness of your industry, goals, and previous inputs. Additionally, by learning from millions of examples, AI assistants recognize common work patterns and offer realistic solutions, making them more effective collaborators than conventional software tools.

2.2.4 Current Capabilities and Limitations

AI assistants excel at generating first drafts of written content, analyzing and summarizing large amounts of information, providing step-by-step guidance for complex tasks, and offering multiple perspectives on problems. Despite these strengths, they also have notable limitations. AI assistants cannot access real-time information unless specifically designed to do so, may produce plausible sounding but incorrect outputs, lack a true understanding of business context and interpersonal relationships, and require human oversight for important decisions. When considering the use of AI in a workday, it is useful to reflect on which tasks might benefit from AI assistance versus those that demand primarily human judgment. For example, tasks that are repetitive, structured, or data-driven are often suitable for AI support, whereas tasks involving nuanced decision-making, ethical considerations, or deep contextual understanding generally require human expertise.

2.3 AI Assistance vs. Human Judgment

Table 2.1: Factors Influencing AI Assistance vs. Human Judgment

Factor	AI Assistance	Human Judgment
Task type	Routine, pattern-based, well-defined	Creative, strategic, relationship-sensitive
Stakes	Low to medium risk, reversible	High stakes, irreversible, ethical implications
Data	Sufficient historical patterns	Limited data, unprecedented situations
Context	Straightforward, objective criteria	Complex interpersonal or cultural factors

Understanding when to rely on AI assistance versus human judgment is essential for working effectively with these tools. AI can be highly effective for tasks that are routine, pattern-based, and well-defined, particularly when sufficient historical data exists to guide decisions. Such tasks are generally low to medium risk and reversible. Examples include generating initial drafts of written content, analyzing large datasets for trends, and providing technical support for coding or documentation. For instance, a sales manager might use AI to create draft email templates for different customer segments and then refine each message using personal knowledge of client relationships. Similarly, a retail analyst could employ AI to identify trending products across regions and then interpret the results using market expertise. In technical problem-solving, a developer might use AI tools like GitHub Copilot to suggest code functions, which are then reviewed and tested to ensure they meet specific project requirements.

Human judgment becomes critical when tasks are creative, strategic, or require sensitivity to relationships, culture, or complex interpersonal dynamics. Decisions that involve high stakes, irreversible consequences, or ethical and legal considerations demand human accountability and moral reasoning. High-pressure or rapidly evolving situations, such as crises, also require human leadership and the ability to act under uncertainty. In these contexts, AI can provide support, but it cannot replace the nuanced decision-making, emotional intelligence, and ethical judgment that humans provide.

It is important to recognize situations in which AI should not be relied upon.

These include high-stakes financial or personnel decisions, tasks involving confidential or sensitive information, complex relationships or cultural considerations, and unprecedented challenges that require innovation. Effective collaboration with AI involves verifying the accuracy of AI-generated outputs, using AI for preliminary drafts or analysis, and then refining and finalizing decisions with human expertise. Transparency about the use of AI and maintaining human oversight for critical decisions are essential for responsible and professional practice.

When reflecting on recent work projects, it can be helpful to identify specific tasks where AI assistance would have been useful and others where human judgment was indispensable. Criteria for these distinctions often include the complexity of the task, the availability of reliable data, the stakes of the decision, and the potential consequences of errors. Recognizing these factors helps ensure that AI is used to complement, rather than replace, human judgment, leading to better outcomes and more ethical decision-making.

2.4 Integration of AI Assistants into Workflows

Successfully integrating AI assistants into business workflows requires rethinking how work gets done. This section provides practical frameworks for incorporating AI assistance into daily operations.

2.4.1 Levels of AI Integration

Table 2.2: Levels of AI Adoption in Organizations

Level	Description	Examples	Complex
Individual use	Personal productivity tools	ChatGPT for writing,Copilot for coding	Low
Team collaboration	Shared AI tools for projects	Meeting summaries,Document editing	Medium

Level	Description	Examples	Complex
Department integration	AI embedded in department workflows	Marketing campaigns,HR recruitment	Medium-high
Enterprise orchestration	Cross-functional AI coordination	Integrated decision-support systems	High

AI can be integrated at multiple levels, ranging from individual use to enterprise-wide orchestration. At the individual level, AI tools enhance personal productivity, such as using ChatGPT for writing or GitHub Copilot for coding. Team-level integration involves shared AI tools to support collaboration, including meeting summaries or document editing. Department-level integration embeds AI into departmental workflows, such as automating marketing campaigns or supporting human resources recruitment. At the enterprise level, AI supports cross-functional coordination through integrated decision-support systems. The table below summarizes these levels:

2.4.2 Integration Patterns

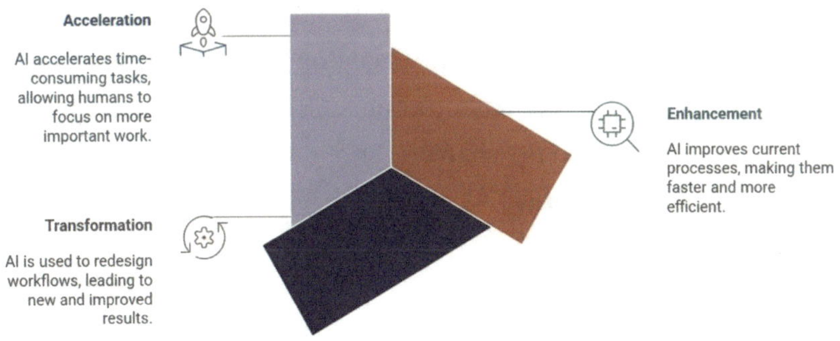

Organizations typically integrate AI using one of three patterns. The enhancement pattern adds AI to existing processes to improve speed and quality without fundamentally changing workflows. For example, a content team might use AI to draft article outlines while retaining their standard editorial process. The transformation pattern involves redesigning workflows around AI capabilities to achieve new outcomes, such as a customer service team shifting from reactive to proactive support using AI predictions. The acceleration pattern leverages AI to dramatically speed up time-intensive tasks, exemplified by a legal team using AI for initial contract review, allowing lawyers to focus on negotiation and strategy.

2.4.3 Practical Implementation Roadmap

Integrating AI into workflows benefits from a phased approach. In weeks one and two, individuals can experiment with AI for routine tasks that consume significant time, documenting improvements in efficiency and quality. In weeks three and four, successful practices should be shared with team members, establishing guidelines for appropriate AI use and developing effective prompts or templates. By the second month, AI can be formally incorporated into team processes, with quality control procedures and training to ensure smooth collaboration. From month three onward, organizations can scale successful applications to related processes, integrate AI with other business systems, and disseminate best practices across teams.

2.4.4 Common Integration Challenges

Several challenges may arise during AI integration. Inconsistent quality can be addressed by developing standardized prompts and quality checklists. Employee resistance can be mitigated by emphasizing that AI augments rather than replaces human work, coupled with training. Information security concerns require clear guidelines for data sharing, and potential workflow disruption can be managed by implementing AI gradually while maintaining parallel processes until reliability is established.

2.5 Applications of AI Assistants in Business

AI assistants are transforming work across every business function. This section explores the most impactful applications with concrete examples and implementation guidance.

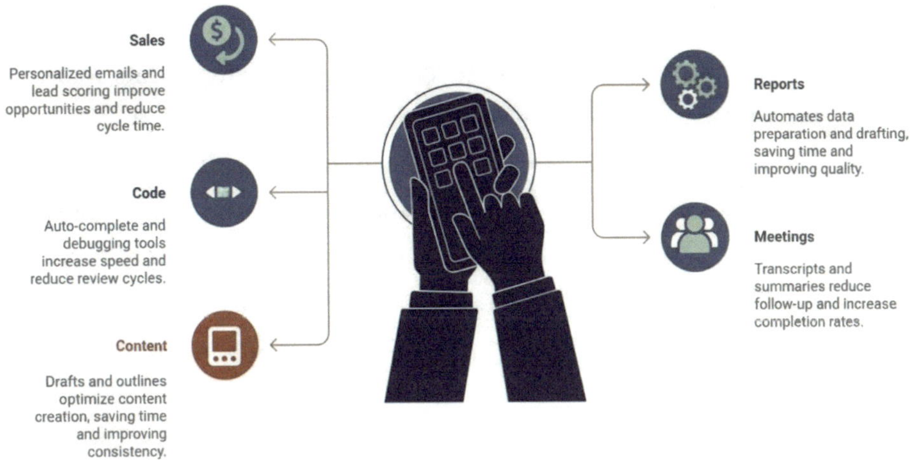

2.5.1 Sales Personalization and Customer Engagement

AI enables mass personalization at scale, revolutionizing how sales teams engage with prospects. It can generate customized emails based on prospect data, automatically create proposals using templates, and analyze behavior to score leads, improving response rates, turnaround times, and conversion. For instance, a software company implemented AI-powered sales assistance that analyzed prospect websites and industry news to generate personalized conversation starters. This resulted in a 35 percent increase in qualified opportunities and a 20 percent reduction in sales cycle length.

2.5.2 Report Generation and Data Analysis

In reporting and data analysis, AI converts raw data into actionable insights, allowing analysts to focus on interpretation and strategic recommendations. Traditional report preparation may take 12 to 17 hours, including data collection, cleaning, analysis, visualization, and writing. With AI, workflows are streamlined: data aggregation, pattern identification, and initial drafting are automated, while humans add business context and refine recommendations. This approach reduces report preparation time by 70 percent, improves consistency and quality by 50 percent, increases insight frequency, and accelerates decision-making by 25 percent.

2.5.3 Productivity and Code Generation

AI coding assistants improve software development efficiency while maintaining quality. They provide auto-completion, function generation, debugging suggestions, and automatic documentation. A fintech startup with fifteen engineers using GitHub Copilot reported a 45 percent increase in feature delivery speed, a 30 percent reduction in code review cycles, and a 50 percent improvement in documentation quality. By handling repetitive coding tasks, AI frees developers to focus on higher-level design, problem-solving, and innovation.

2.5.4 Meeting Summaries and Documentation

AI transforms how organizations capture and act on meeting information. Traditional meetings rely on manual notetaking, which is often incomplete and time-consuming to organize, resulting in lost action items and inconsistent documentation. AI now provides automatic transcription, summarization, action item identification, and searchable archives. Tools such as Otter.ai, Read.ai, and Microsoft Copilot enable real-time transcription, summary generation, and integration with enterprise collaboration platforms. Organizations using these tools report up to an 80 percent reduction in follow-up time, a 60 percent improvement in action item completion, and increased meeting productivity, with participants strongly preferring AI-generated summaries over manual notes.

2.5.5 Content Creation and Marketing

AI enhances marketing workflows by enabling faster content creation while maintaining brand consistency. AI can generate ideas, create outlines, draft content, and optimize messaging, while humans contribute expertise, insights, and relationship knowledge. For example, the process of producing a blog post can be reduced from 15 to 23 hours to just 5 to 7 hours by combining AI efficiency with human refinement. Effective implementation balances AI-generated content with human creativity and judgment, ensuring output is both scalable and authentic.

2.6 Conclusion

AI assistants are transforming the way work is done by shifting the focus from learning a computer's language to having computers understand human intent. These tools function as collaborative partners, augmenting human capabilities and creating opportunities to leverage both artificial and human intelligence. They excel at handling routine, pattern-based tasks with clear criteria, allowing humans to concentrate on high-stakes decisions, complex relationships, and ethical considerations. Maintaining human oversight is essential to ensure accuracy, accountability, and responsible use.

Effective integration of AI into workflows is gradual and strategic. It begins with improving individual productivity and then scales to team and organizational processes. The focus should be on enhancing existing workflows rather than attempting to replace them entirely, allowing users to build confidence and capability over time. When applied appropriately, AI assistants deliver measurable value across business functions, from accelerating coding and data analysis to reducing report preparation time. The common thread is using AI for routine cognitive work while freeing humans for strategic thinking, problem-solving, and relationship-building.

Thriving in an AI-augmented workplace requires developing a set of essential skills. Prompt engineering, or communicating effectively with AI systems, is critical, as is the ability to critically evaluate AI output for accuracy and relevance. Professionals must structure workflows that leverage both AI efficiency and human expertise and exercise sound ethical reasoning when making decisions involving AI. This shift also demands a mindset evolution, moving from "doing the work" to "directing the work," from trying to know everything to knowing how to evaluate information, and from focusing solely on individual productivity to optimizing human-AI collaboration.

Chapter 3

APIs and System Integration

3.1 Introduction

Imagine your smartphone automatically updating your calendar when you book a flight, your fitness tracker syncing with your health app, and your music streaming service knowing your preferences across all devices. This seamless connectivity doesn't happen by magic – it's powered by APIs (Application Programming Interfaces), the invisible bridges that allow different software systems to communicate and share data.

In the business world, APIs serve as the digital nervous system that connects everything from customer relationship management (CRM) systems to financial dashboards, inventory management to customer support platforms. They enable the automated workflows that modern businesses depend on, allowing data to flow seamlessly between systems without human intervention.

Consider a simple online purchase: when you buy something, APIs automatically update inventory levels, process payment, generate shipping labels, send confirmation emails, and update customer records across multiple systems – all in seconds. This level of integration has transformed how businesses operate, enabling real-time decision-making and automated responses that would be impossible with manual processes.

The rise of AI assistants has made API integration even more powerful. These intelligent systems can now access data from multiple business systems, analyze patterns, and trigger automated actions across your entire technology stack. A customer service AI might pull information from your CRM, check inventory levels, process a refund, and update support tickets – all through API connections.

This chapter will demystify APIs and system integration, showing you how these technologies enable the automated, data-driven businesses of today. We'll explore practical examples from CRM updates to financial dashboards and learn how AI assistants leverage APIs to create truly intelligent automation workflows.

3.2 APIs and Their Role in Automation

3.2.1 What is an API?

An API (Application Programming Interface) is essentially a messenger that allows two software applications to talk to each other. Think of it as a waiter in a restaurant: you (one application) tell the waiter (API) what you want from the kitchen (another application), and the waiter brings back exactly what you requested.

In technical terms, an API defines the methods, data formats, and rules that applications use to communicate. But for business purposes, APIs are simply the technology that makes automation possible by allowing different systems to share information and trigger actions automatically.

3.2.2 APIs in Everyday Business Operations

APIs, or Application Programming Interfaces, enable different software systems to communicate and work together seamlessly. Consider the example of online shopping. When you place an order, multiple APIs coordinate the process behind the scenes. The shopping cart API sends payment information to the payment processor API, ensuring secure transactions. Simultaneously, the order API communicates with the inventory system API to update stock levels. Shipping details are transmitted to a logistics API to generate labels, while the order API also triggers the email API to send confirmation messages to the customer. Finally, all transaction data flows to analytics APIs for reporting and insight generation. This entire sequence occurs in seconds without any human intervention, illustrating how APIs streamline business operations and integrate systems efficiently.

3.2.3 The Four Types of Business APIs Business

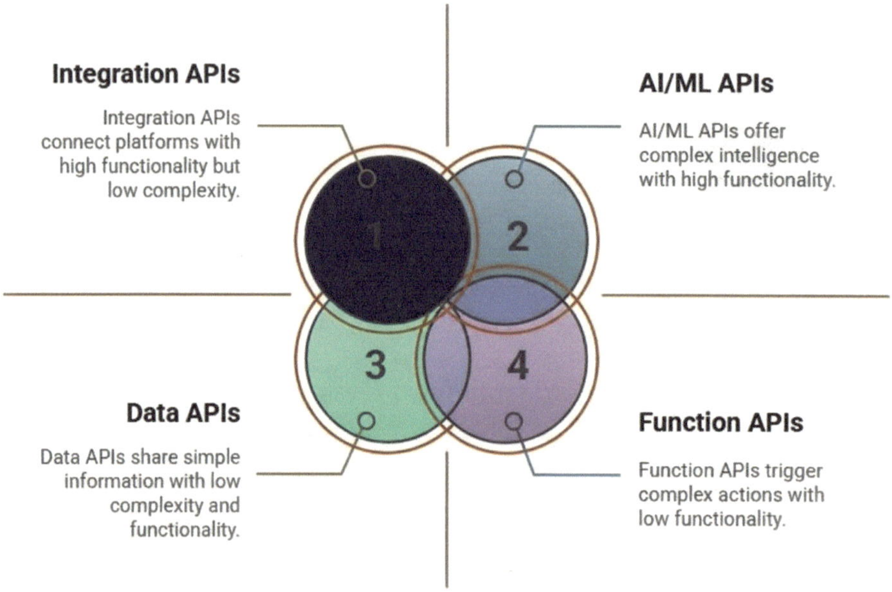

APIs can be categorized into four main types, each serving distinct purposes and adding specific value to operations. Data APIs allow systems to share information, such as customer records or product catalogs, providing real-time access to critical business data. Function APIs trigger specific actions, like sending emails or processing payments, automating routine tasks and reducing manual effort. Integration APIs connect different platforms—for example, linking a CRM system to marketing automation software—helping eliminate data silos and ensuring seamless workflows across departments. Finally, AI/ML APIs add intelligent capabilities to existing systems, such as language translation or image recognition, enhancing products and services with advanced AI features. Together, these four types of APIs enable organizations to streamline operations, improve efficiency, and build smarter, more connected systems.

3.2.4 How APIs Enable Automation

In a traditional, manual workflow, processing a customer order involves multiple steps that require human intervention. An employee receives the order notification, manually checks the inventory system, processes the payment in a separate system, updates the customer record in the CRM, creates a shipping label in the logistics system, and sends a confirmation email. This entire process can take between 15 and 30 minutes per order. In contrast, an API-automated workflow triggers an order-based workflow where APIs simultaneously handle all system updates, including inventory, payment, CRM records, shipping, and customer notifications. Human oversight is only needed for exceptions or errors, reducing the total processing time to around 30 seconds per order. The key insight is that APIs do more than accelerate existing processes—they enable entirely new business models by allowing real-time, automated responses at scale.

3.2.5 API Security and Business Considerations

Ensuring the security of APIs is critical for protecting business data and maintaining trust in automated systems. Common authentication methods include API keys, which function like simple passwords for system access; OAuth, which provides secure authorization for user data; and JWT tokens, which use encrypted credentials for sensitive operations. Secure APIs offer several business benefits, such as controlled access to confidential information, audit trails for compliance and monitoring, the ability to revoke access when necessary, and protection against unauthorized system usage. Best practices for API security include implementing rate limiting to prevent system overload, encrypting sensitive data, performing regular security audits and updates, and establishing clear access permissions for different types of users. Together, these measures ensure that APIs operate safely and reliably while enabling efficient, automated business processes.

Common Integration Patterns Between Business Systems

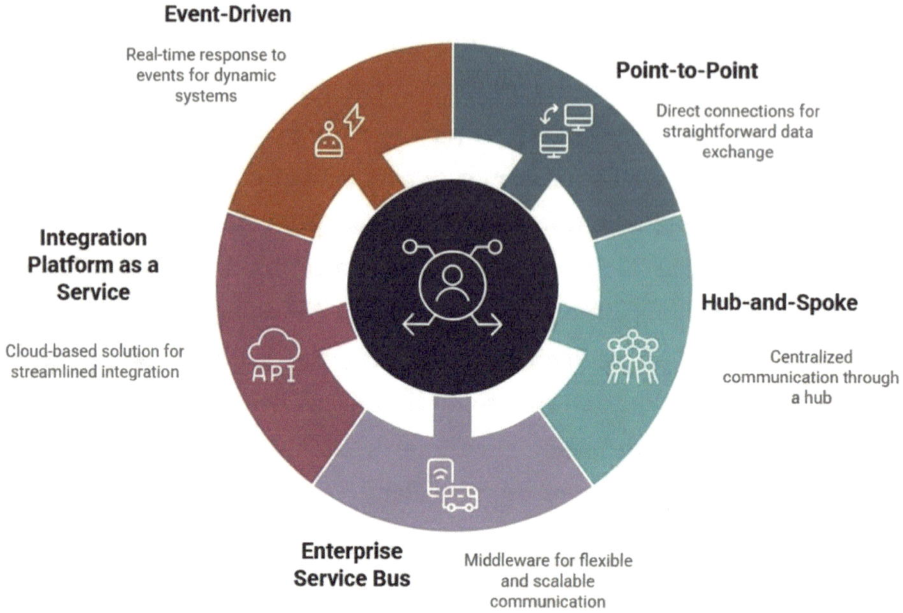

Understanding how business systems connect is essential for identifying automation opportunities and designing efficient workflows. Integration patterns describe standardized approaches to linking systems, allowing information to flow seamlessly and processes to be coordinated effectively. Choosing the right pattern depends on factors such as the number of systems involved, data synchronization frequency, technical expertise, scalability needs, and budget constraints.

Point-to-Point Integration

One of the simplest approaches is point-to-point integration, in which two specific systems are directly connected. This method is best suited for low-volume, critical system connections, such as linking a CRM to an email marketing platform. Point-to-point integrations are fast to implement and easy to understand, but as the number of systems grows, the network of connections can become complex and difficult to maintain.

Hub-and-Spoke Integration

Hub-and-spoke integration centralizes communication through a single hub, which manages all connections between systems. This approach works well for organizations that need multiple systems to share data, such as an ERP system connecting to CRM, inventory, and accounting platforms. Hub-and-spoke integration offers centralized control and easier management, though the hub can become a single point of failure if not properly maintained.

Enterprise Service Bus (ESB)

For large organizations with many complex systems, Enterprise Service Bus (ESB) provides a robust middleware layer to handle communication. ESBs are highly scalable and offer sophisticated error handling, making them suitable for environments like banking systems that link loans, deposits, and customer service platforms. However, ESBs are complex to implement and maintain, requiring significant technical expertise.

Cloud Integration Platforms (iPaaS)

Cloud-based solutions, known as integration platforms as a service (iPaaS), offer flexible, scalable connections between multiple systems. Platforms such as Zapier allow growing businesses to integrate hundreds of applications quickly using pre-built connectors. While iPaaS solutions are easy to set up and maintain, they involve subscription costs and may create vendor dependency.

Event-Driven Integration

Event-driven integration enables systems to respond automatically to specific events or triggers. This pattern is ideal for real-time business needs, such as automatically creating follow-up tasks when a support ticket is generated. Event-driven integration improves responsiveness and efficiency but requires careful design and can be challenging to debug.

Comparing Integration Patterns

Integration patterns can be compared in terms of setup complexity, maintenance, scalability, and suitability. Point-to-point setups are low in complexity and maintenance but scale poorly beyond a few systems. Hub-and-spoke integration offers moderate complexity and better scalability, while ESBs provide enterprise-scale performance at the cost of higher complexity. iPaaS solutions combine low setup effort with excellent scalability for growing businesses, and event-driven architectures deliver real-time responsiveness for time-sensitive operations.

Real-World Examples

Real-world examples illustrate the practical application of these patterns. In e-commerce, a customer placing an order triggers a series of API calls: inventory is checked, payment is processed, shipping labels are generated, CRM records are updated, confirmation emails are sent, and analytics data is captured. In professional services firms, completing a project milestone can automatically calculate billable hours, generate invoices, update client records in the CRM, record revenue in accounting systems, and refresh reporting dashboards. These examples demonstrate how integration patterns enable streamlined, automated workflows across complex business environments.

Selecting the Right Integration Approach

Selecting the right integration approach requires careful assessment. Organizations should start simple by evaluating the number of systems to connect, the frequency of data synchronization, technical expertise, and budget. Growth planning is equally important: anticipate additional systems, determine whether real-time or periodic data synchronization is needed, and consider critical uptime, compliance, and security requirements. Warning signs of inadequate integration include manual data transfers, file exchanges via email, and delays in obtaining updated information.

Measuring Integration Success

Integration success should be measured using both technical and business metrics. Technical metrics include data synchronization accuracy, system uptime, API response times, and error rates, while business metrics focus on time saved, reduction of data errors, faster decision-making, and improvements in customer experience. By carefully choosing integration patterns, planning for growth, and monitoring outcomes, organizations can design workflows that are efficient, reliable, and scalable.

3.3 Real-Time vs. Batch Data Flows

In business automation, understanding when to use real-time versus batch data processing is essential for designing effective workflows. Each approach has distinct advantages and is suited to different operational needs, and choosing the right method affects speed, efficiency, cost, and overall business outcomes.

3.3.1 The Fundamental Difference

Real-time processing handles data immediately as it arrives, enabling instant responses and up-to-the-minute information. Batch processing, on the other hand, collects data over time and processes it in groups at scheduled intervals. This approach is more efficient for large volumes of data and complex analytical tasks.

3.3.2 Comparing Real-Time and Batch Processing

Table 3.1: Real-Time Processing vs. Batch Processing

Aspect	Real-time processing	Batch processing
Speed	Immediate (milliseconds–seconds)	Delayed (minutes–hours)
Resource usage	Continuous, higher overhead	Periodic, efficient
Complexity	Higher technical complexity	Simpler to implement
Cost	Higher operational costs	Lower operational costs
Use cases	Fraud detection, Live dashboards	Reports, Analytics, Backups

3.3.2.1 When to Use Real-Time Processing

Real-time processing is critical when speed directly impacts the customer experience, safety, or business decisions. In financial services, it enables credit card fraud detection, instant balance updates, and real-time stock trading. In e-commerce, real-time processing ensures inventory is updated instantly, pricing adapts dynamically to demand, and product recommendations reflect current browsing behavior. In customer service, live chat systems, immediate ticket routing, and real-time sentiment analysis allow companies to respond to client needs without delay.

3.3.2.2 When to Use Batch Processing

Batch processing is best for managing large amounts of data efficiently, especially when immediate action is not required. It supports financial reporting, regulatory compliance, and large-scale customer billing by consolidating data from multiple sources. Marketing teams use batch processing to analyze campaign performance, update customer segmentation, and prepare mass email campaigns. Operations teams leverage it for inventory planning, payroll processing, and systematic data backups. This approach optimizes resource use and ensures consistency over speed.

3.3.2.3 Hybrid Approaches

Many businesses combine real-time and batch processing to take advantage of both methods. E-commerce platforms may use real-time workflows for inventory updates, payment processing, and customer notifications while relying on batch processing for daily sales reports, monthly customer analytics, and quarterly financial statements. Similarly, banking systems use real-time processing for transactions and fraud detection while performing interest calculations, monthly statements, and regulatory reporting in batches.

3.3.3 Implementation Considerations

Real-time processing requires a robust infrastructure capable of 24/7 operation, continuous monitoring, alerting systems, and backup mechanisms. It also demands higher technical expertise to maintain performance and reliability. Batch processing requires scheduled job management, data quality validation, error handling, and sufficient storage for temporary and processed datasets.

3.3.3.1 Cost and Value Comparison

Combining both methods often produces the best results. Real-time processing is most valuable for operational tasks where immediacy is critical, while batch processing provides insights and efficiency for analytical tasks. Choosing the appropriate method requires understanding business requirements, assessing technical capabilities, evaluating costs, and considering future data needs. Common mistakes include implementing real-time unnecessarily, relying on batch for time-sensitive tasks, ignoring future growth in data volume, and neglecting monitoring and error handling.

3.4 How AI Assistants Access and Manipulate Operational Data

AI assistants are transforming business operations by accessing, analyzing, and acting on data from multiple systems. By integrating with business infrastructure, these intelligent systems enable truly automated workflows that reduce manual effort, increase accuracy, and provide real-time insights for decision-making.

3.4.1 How AI Assistants Connect to Business Systems

Modern AI assistants typically follow an API-first architecture, connecting directly to business systems. This allows them to read data, trigger actions, and update records across multiple platforms simultaneously. Integration can occur at three levels. In the read-only level, AI assistants can view and analyze data to generate reports or answer questions, providing insights and analysis. At the action-enabled level, AI triggers predefined workflows such as sending emails or creating support tickets, automating routine processes. Full integration allows AI to read, analyze, and modify data directly, updating records and making decisions to achieve intelligent automation. : Levels of AI System Access and Integration {#tbl-ai-access-levels width=80%}

Level	Capability	Examples	Business impact
Read-only access	View and analyze data	Generate reports, Answer questions	Insights and analysis
Action-enabled	Trigger predefined workflows	Send emails, Create tickets	Process automation
Full integration	Read, analyze, and modify data	Update records, Make decisions	Intelligent automation

AI assistants access data using different patterns. The query pattern involves asking for specific information, such as sales numbers for a particular quarter. The analysis pattern combines data from multiple sources to generate actionable insights, like combining sales, customer feedback, and market trends to recommend pricing changes. The trigger pattern monitors systems and automatically responds to specific conditions, such as detecting low inventory levels and creating purchase orders. Finally, the workflow pattern allows AI to orchestrate complex processes across multiple systems, managing end-to-end operations like customer onboarding from initial contact to account setup.

3.4.2 Real-World AI Integration Examples

3.4.2.1 CRM Updates and Customer Management

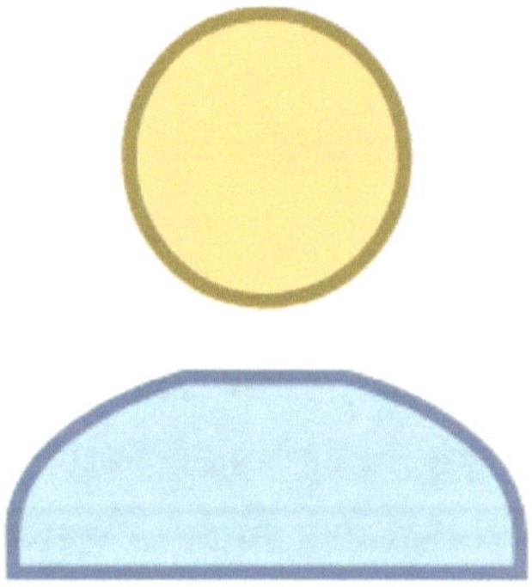

Traditional CRM workflows often require sales reps to manually enter customer information, update opportunity status, schedule follow-ups, and export data to create reports. AI assistants streamline these processes by listening to sales calls, automatically updating CRM records, analyzing conversation sentiment, scheduling follow-up activities, and generating real-time insights and recommendations. By connecting to CRM APIs, using natural language processing, and applying machine learning models, AI reduces manual data entry by 75 percent, improves data accuracy by 40 percent, and increases sales productivity by 25 percent.

3.4.2.2 Financial Dashboards and Real-Time Analytics

AI assistants provide real-time financial intelligence by connecting to accounting systems, bank APIs, and payment processors. They perform automated variance analysis, cash flow forecasting, expense categorization, and anomaly detection. The integration flow from AI assistant to accounting and banking APIs enables real-time dashboards showing cash position, pending receivables, expense trends, and profitability. Businesses gain daily financial insights instead of relying on monthly reports, achieve a 60 percent faster month-end closing process, and can proactively manage cash flow while automating compliance and audit preparation.

3.4.2.3 Automated Inventory Management

AI assistants optimize inventory by monitoring stock levels across locations, predicting demand, and managing reordering processes. Using sales history, seasonal trends, and market data, AI forecasts demand, triggers purchase orders at optimal reorder points, evaluates supplier options, and monitors product quality. By integrating warehouse management and procurement APIs, AI reduces stockouts by 30 percent, decreases excess inventory by 25 percent, and halves the time spent on manual ordering, while improving supplier performance through data-driven decision-making.

3.4.2.4 Customer Support Integration

Intelligent AI can automate customer service by accessing CRM records, product databases, order management systems, and support knowledge bases. When a customer submits a request, AI analyzes the query and customer history, categorizes and prioritizes tickets, provides initial responses, routes complex issues to humans, and updates records with resolution details. Advanced features include sentiment analysis to detect frustration, predictive support for potential issues, personalized communication, and cross-selling opportunities. This integration improves response times, enhances customer experience, and reduces manual workload for support teams.

3.4.3 Security and Compliance Considerations

AI access to operational data requires strong security measures. All API connections should be encrypted, with role-based access controls and audit trails to track AI actions and decisions. Regular security assessments and updates are critical. Compliance with GDPR, SOX, HIPAA, PCI-DSS, and other industry-specific regulations must be maintained, along with clear data retention and deletion policies. Best practices include applying least-privilege access principles, monitoring AI activities continuously, documenting AI decision-making processes, and ensuring human oversight for high-stakes decisions.

Although AI assistants can access and manipulate operational data effectively, human oversight remains essential for decisions that involve significant financial impact, customer relationships, or ethical considerations. AI should augment, not replace, human judgment in critical business operations.

3.5 Conclusion

APIs have become the digital backbone of modern businesses, enabling seamless communication between systems and transforming manual, time-consuming processes into automated workflows that operate in seconds rather than hours. They allow organizations to respond more quickly to customers, markets, and operational challenges. Choosing the right integration approach—whether point-to-point, hub-and-spoke, ESB, iPaaS, or event-driven architecture—depends on business size, technical capabilities, and growth plans, with simple solutions often providing the best balance of functionality and complexity for emerging organizations. Similarly, deciding between real-time and batch processing should be guided by business needs: real-time for customer-facing speed and batch for efficiency and cost-effectiveness, with many businesses successfully using both.

The next evolution in integration involves AI-powered systems. AI assistants can analyze data across multiple systems, identify patterns, and trigger appropriate actions, enabling intelligent automation and proactive decision-making. Businesses progress along an integration maturity journey, beginning with manual processes prone to errors and slow response times, advancing through basic

API connections and automated data flows, and ultimately reaching intelligent automation and adaptive systems that optimize themselves over time while facilitating seamless human-AI collaboration.

Organizations can future-proof their integration strategies by beginning with business requirements, designing for scalable expansion, emphasizing security via robust authentication and encryption, and keeping human supervision so that AI supports rather than overtakes human decision-making. Emerging trends such as low-code/no-code integration, event-driven architectures, AI-native systems, and edge computing are shaping the next generation of responsive, intelligent operations.

Building integration competency requires a combination of technical and business skills, including API literacy, data flow design, security awareness, and business process analysis. Practical steps for developing these skills include experimenting with simple API integrations using tools like Zapier or Microsoft Power Automate, mapping current or target data flows, practicing how to explain technical concepts in business terms, and staying current with evolving integration platforms and AI capabilities. By understanding APIs, integration strategies, and the role of AI, professionals can create more efficient, intelligent, and agile business systems that deliver measurable value and support long-term growth.

Chapter 4

Automated Analytics and Reporting

4.1 Introduction

Imagine walking into your office on Monday morning and finding a personalized report waiting for you that not only summarizes last week's performance but also predicts this week's challenges and recommends specific actions to take. This report has automatically gathered data from dozens of systems, identified the most important trends, and even flagged potential problems before they become critical. This isn't a fantasy – it's how leading organizations are already using automated analytics and AI-powered reporting.

Traditional business reporting often feels like looking in the rearview mirror while driving. By the time you see the data, analyze the trends, and make decisions, market conditions have already changed. Automated analytics flips this paradigm, providing real-time insights and forward-looking intelligence that enables proactive decision-making.

The transformation is remarkable. Companies using automated analytics reports to reduce report preparation time by 70% while increasing the frequency and quality of insights. More importantly, they're shifting from reactive to predictive management, identifying opportunities and threats before competitors even recognize they exist.

Consider Netflix's approach to content decisions. Instead of waiting for quarterly reviews, their automated analytics continuously monitor viewing patterns, predict audience preferences, and recommend content investments in real-time. This system processes billions of data points daily, generating insights that would take traditional analysts months to uncover.

This chapter will guide you through the three levels of automated analytics – descriptive (what happened), predictive (what will happen), and prescriptive (what should we do) – and show you how AI transforms each level from manual, time-intensive processes into intelligent, automated systems that enhance human decision-making.

4.2 How AI Automates Analytics

Understanding how AI enhances analytics at different levels is essential for designing effective automated reporting systems. Analytics builds from descriptive to predictive to prescriptive insights, with each level providing increasingly sophisticated decision-support capabilities.

4.2.1 The Analytics Hierarchy

Analytics can be categorized into three levels. Descriptive analytics focuses on understanding what has happened by summarizing historical data and current performance. Predictive analytics examine patterns to forecast what is likely to happen in the future. Prescriptive analytics provides actionable recommendations to optimize business decisions and outcomes. Each level builds on the previous one, enabling progressively deeper insights and automation.

4.2.1.1 Descriptive Analytics: AI-Powered Historical Insights

Traditional descriptive analytics often require manual collection of data from multiple sources. Reports are usually static, generated weekly or monthly, and consist of basic charts and tables. Analysts must interpret the data to discover trends, and the ability to drill down into details is limited. AI enhances descriptive analytics by automating data aggregation from all connected systems. Real-time dashboards update continuously, natural language summaries explain key trends, and interactive visualizations allow intelligent filtering of information. : Traditional vs. AI-Enhanced Data Capabilities {#tbl-traditional-vs-ai width=80%}

Capability	Traditional approach	AI-enhanced approach
Data collection	Manual exports and imports	Automated API connections
Report generation	Hours of manual work	Minutes of automated processing
Insight discovery	Analyst interpretation required	AI identifies key patterns automatically
Update frequency	Weekly or monthly	Real-time or hourly
Accessibility	Technical skills required	Natural language queries

For example, a sales manager may spend four hours every Monday morning collecting data from CRM systems, spreadsheets, and emails to create a weekly sales summary. An AI-enhanced system continuously monitors all sales channels, generates real-time performance summaries, and delivers personalized insights to each manager, highlighting team achievements and areas needing attention.

4.2.1.2 Predictive Analytics: AI-Powered Forecasting

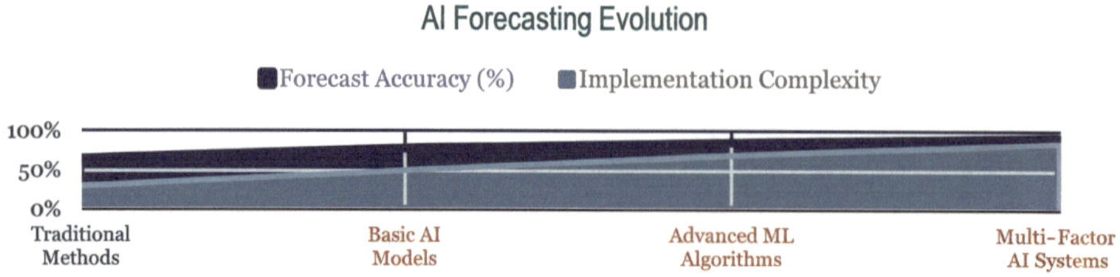

Predictive analytics uses historical and current data to forecast future outcomes. AI improves prediction by identifying complex patterns across multiple variables that humans might overlook. Key AI capabilities include recognizing subtle correlations, adjusting for seasonal patterns, integrating external factors such as market trends or weather, providing confidence intervals rather than single-point predictions, and continuously improving accuracy as more data becomes available.

Table 4.2: Traditional vs. AI-Enhanced Business Forecasting

Business function	Traditional forecasting	AI-enhanced prediction
Sales	Linear trend projection	Multi-factor demand modeling with market intelligence
Inventory	Safety stock calculations	Dynamic optimization based on demand patterns
Finance	Budget variance analysis	Cash flow forecasting with scenario modeling
Marketing	Campaign ROI estimates	Customer lifetime value and churn prediction
Operations	Capacity planning	Predictive maintenance and resource optimization

For instance, a mid-sized retailer implemented AI-powered demand forecasting that analyzes sales history, weather patterns, local events, and social media trends. The results included a 35% reduction in stockouts, a 25% decrease in excess inventory, a 40% improvement in forecast accuracy, and $2 million in annual savings from optimized purchasing.

4.2.1.3 Prescriptive Analytics: AI-Powered Decision Recommendations

Prescriptive analytics goes beyond prediction by recommending specific actions. AI evaluates multiple possible scenarios, simulates outcomes, identifies optimal strategies, assesses potential risks, and provides actionable plans. An e-commerce company, for example, may optimize pricing for 10,000 products daily using AI. The system analyzes competitor pricing, demand elasticity, inventory levels, and customer segments to generate optimal prices and continuously adjusts strategy based on results. This approach produced a 15% increase in revenue and an 8% improvement in profit margins.

Similarly, a marketing team may rely on AI to allocate a $500,000 budget across multiple channels. AI analyzes historical campaign performance, predicts ROI for various allocation scenarios, and recommends the optimal distribution and timing of spend. This method led to a 45% improvement in campaign ROI and a 30% increase in qualified leads.

4.2.2 Making Analytics Actionable

Implementing AI-powered analytics successfully requires careful integration into business workflows. Common challenges include producing insights without actionable plans, maintaining siloed analytics across departments, over-automating decisions that require human judgment, and creating an overwhelming volume of information. Best practices involve defining business questions before building analytics models, ensuring that insights are linked to specific actions, maintaining human oversight for critical decisions, and continuously refining models based on actual outcomes. When applied thoughtfully, AI-powered analytics transforms descriptive, predictive, and prescriptive insights into meaningful business decisions that improve efficiency, accuracy, and strategic impact.

4.3 Automated Data Collection, Analysis, and Dynamic Reporting

Effective automated analytics depends on seamlessly collecting data from multiple sources, analyzing it intelligently, and presenting insights in formats that drive action. Modern AI systems transform the entire data-to-decision pipeline, reducing manual effort and enabling real-time business intelligence.

4.3.1 The Automated Data Pipeline

In traditional data workflows, preparing a report can take between twelve and twenty hours. Analysts manually extract data from various systems, spend several hours cleaning and formatting it, perform analysis, create visualizations, write and format reports, and distribute findings for follow-up. In contrast, an AI-automated workflow collects data continuously through APIs, validates and cleans it in real time, detects patterns automatically, generates dynamic reports with actionable insights, and distributes personalized alerts. The result is minutes, rather than hours, to deliver meaningful insights.

4.3.2 Automated Data Collection Strategies

Modern businesses generate data across numerous systems, making multi-source integration essential. Transactional systems such as CRM, ERP, and point-of-sale platforms feed real-time data through APIs continuously. Marketing platforms, including Google Analytics and social media tools, provide data through scheduled API connections, updated hourly or daily. External data sources such as market reports, weather feeds, and news are collected as available via third-party APIs. File-based systems, including spreadsheets and other reports, can be uploaded automatically on a daily or weekly schedule.

IoT devices and sensors supply streaming data that updates in real time.

Data quality automation is another critical capability. AI systems can automatically detect and correct common issues, including duplicate records, missing values, unusual outliers, inconsistent formatting, and violations of business validation rules. By ensuring clean and reliable data, AI lays the foundation for trustworthy analytics.

Table 4.3: Data Sources, Collection Methods, and Update Frequencies

Data source type	Examples	Collection method	Update frequency
Transactional systems	CRM, ERP, POS	Real-time APIs	Continuous
Marketing platforms	Google Analytics, Social Media	Scheduled APIs	Hourly/Daily
External data	Market data, Weather, News	Third-party APIs	As available
File-based systems	Spreadsheets, Reports	Automated uploads	Daily/Weekly
IoT and sensors	Equipment data, Location	Streaming data	Real-time

4.3.3 Intelligent Analysis Automation

AI excels at recognizing patterns at scale, identifying insights that would be impossible for humans to detect manually, especially across complex datasets. Anomaly detection allows AI to spot unusual behavior, adapt to seasonal or cyclical patterns, provide context for why values are flagged, and suggest potential causes and recommended actions. For example, an e-commerce system may detect a 40% drop in mobile conversion rates, trace the issue to a website update, and alert the development team with detailed error information.

Trend analysis identifies emerging patterns before they become obvious, separates meaningful signals from noise in volatile data, provides confidence levels for predictions, and recommends optimal timing for business responses. A retail analytics system may detect early increases in demand for outdoor equipment and suggest inventory adjustments weeks before competitors notice the trend.

Segmentation and clustering enable AI to group customers, products, or behaviors automatically. New segments are detected as they emerge, actionable insights are provided for each segment, and the evolution of each group is tracked over time. For instance, a marketing system might identify a new segment of "eco-conscious millennials" and automatically generate targeted campaign recommendations.

4.3.4 Dynamic Reporting Revolution

Traditional reports become outdated immediately after they are created. Dynamic reporting ensures that insights are continuously updated and adaptive to changing conditions. Personalized dashboards provide customized views for different roles, adjusting layouts based on user behavior and preferences. They highlight contextual insights relevant to current business priorities and are optimized for mobile access. Natural language generation allows AI to create plain-English summaries of key findings, explain complex statistical results, and provide automated storytelling that connects data points to business outcomes. Real-time updates ensure live feeds reflect current business conditions, forecasts are recalculated automatically, alerts are issued when significant changes occur, and historical context is included to help users understand performance trends.

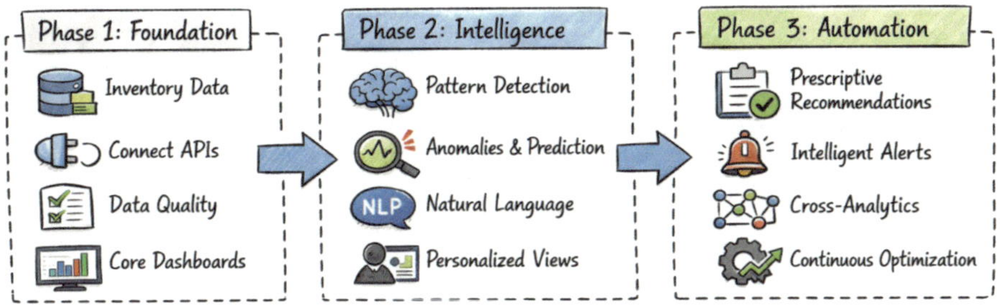

Implementing automated analytics typically occurs in three phases. In the first phase, organizations inventory all data sources, establish API connections to critical systems, implement basic data quality processes, and create initial automated dashboards for key metrics. The second phase introduces the intelligence layer, deploying AI models for pattern recognition, anomaly detection, predictive analytics, natural language insights, and personalized reporting views. The final phase adds advanced automation, integrating prescriptive analytics, recommendation engines, intelligent alert prioritization, cross-functional analytics, and performance optimizations based on user feedback.

4.3.5 Measuring Success and ROI

Effectiveness is measured using efficiency, business impact, and user experience metrics. Efficiency improvements include the reduction of time spent on report preparation, increasing insight delivery frequency from weekly to real-time, improving data accuracy, and promoting adoption across business functions. Business impact is measured by faster decision-making, improved forecast accuracy, increased revenue from data-driven decisions, and cost savings from operational efficiencies. User experience metrics evaluate how quickly users can find relevant information, satisfaction with report quality, reduction in ad-hoc requests to IT, and adoption of self-service analytics.

4.4 Designing Alert Systems for Key Business Metrics

Effective alert systems transform automated analytics from passive reporting tools into active business intelligence that drives immediate action. Intelligent alert systems are designed to inform decision-makers without overwhelming them and to prioritize critical issues while ensuring nothing important is missing.

4.4.1 The Alert System Hierarchy

Alerts are often categorized into three levels based on urgency and potential business impact. Critical alerts require immediate action and involve issues that could significantly affect operations, customer experience, or financial performance. Warning alerts indicate trends or patterns that need monitoring and potential intervention within hours or days. Informational alerts serve to raise awareness about positive developments, milestone achievements, or routine status updates.

4.4.2 Principles of Smart Alert Design

Modern AI alert systems move beyond fixed threshold notifications by incorporating business context and adaptive intelligence. Traditional alerting often relies on static numeric limits, immediate notifications, and equal weighting of all alerts, which can lead to fatigue and reduced responsiveness. AI-enhanced alert systems adjust thresholds dynamically based on historical patterns and business cycles, schedule alerts intelligently according to urgency, and provide context about the potential impact of each alert. Alerts are prioritized by importance, and frequency is adapted to prevent overload while ensuring that critical issues are never missed.

4.4.3 Critical Business Metrics and Alert Categories

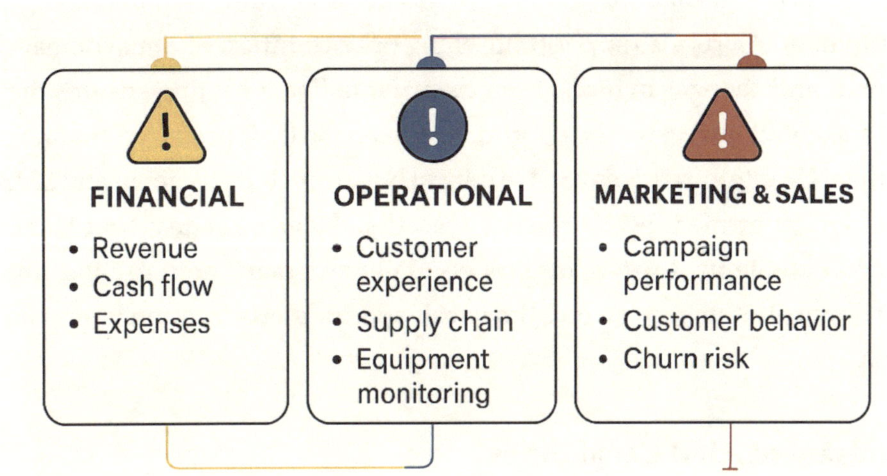

Financial performance alerts monitor key metrics such as revenue, cash flow, and expenses. For example, a daily revenue variance alert could be triggered if revenue falls below 85 percent of the forecast and trends downward for three consecutive days. Alerts of this type are classified as critical if the variance exceeds 25 percent or as a warning if between 15 and 25 percent. The alert is routed to the CFO, sales director, and CEO with a requirement to investigate and implement corrective actions within four hours. In practice, a SaaS company's automated financial alerts identified a 20 percent drop in new subscriptions three days before a board meeting, uncovering a payment processing issue and preventing a $50,000 revenue loss.

Operational performance alerts cover customer experience, supply chain intelligence, and equipment monitoring. These alerts can detect website performance degradation, delayed customer service response times, product quality issues, inventory stockouts, supplier delivery delays, and capacity utilization approaching limits. Predictive maintenance alerts, for instance, provide a 48-hour advance warning of potential equipment failures, automatically generate work orders, recommend parts ordering, and help evaluate repair versus replacement decisions. One manufacturing company achieved a 60 percent reduction in unplanned downtime and a 30 percent decrease in maintenance costs using such a system.

Marketing and sales alerts monitor campaign performance and customer behavior. AI systems can identify drops in conversion rates, increased cost per acquisition, lead quality degradation, competitive threats, and churn risk among high-value customers. Alerts also support upselling opportunities, seasonal demand adjustments, and changes in market sentiment. Intelligent routing ensures that different stakeholders receive the appropriate alerts via their preferred channels. For example, C-suite executives receive critical business alerts by email and SMS immediately, department heads receive operational alerts via dashboards and email within one hour, team managers get daily summary notifications, and individual contributors receive real-time, task-specific alerts through in-app notifications.

4.4.4 Advanced Alert Capabilities

Predictive alerting enables AI to forecast potential problems and notify stakeholders before issues become critical. In customer churn prevention, AI analyzes behavior patterns, support interactions, and usage trends to identify customers with a high likelihood of leaving. Account managers are automatically alerted with specific retention recommendations, and the system continuously refines its predictive accuracy over time.

Contextual intelligence enhances alert utility by providing actionable information, not just notifications. Smart alert components may include root cause analysis to investigate why the alert was triggered, impact assessment to estimate business consequences, recommended actions with suggested steps to resolve the issue, historical context showing similar situations, and success probability for different resolution approaches.

4.4.5 Implementation Best Practices

Successful implementation starts with simplicity and scales strategically. Organizations should begin by identifying the top five critical metrics that drive immediate business value, assign clear ownership for each alert type, define standard response protocols, and continuously measure and optimize alert effectiveness. Common pitfalls include over-alerting, sending alerts without sufficient context, poor timing of notifications, and lack of follow-up to ensure appropriate actions are taken.

4.4.6 Measuring ROI of Alert Systems

Quantitative metrics for alert system effectiveness include response time from alert to action, the rate of false positives, the number of issues prevented before impacting customers, and financial savings from early problem detection. Qualitative benefits include increased confidence among decision-makers, reduced stress from unexpected issues, improved adherence to service level agreements, and enhanced work-life balance through intelligent alert timing. Together, these measures ensure that AI-driven alerts support proactive, informed decision-making across the organization.

4.5 Real-World Applications

This section demonstrates how automated analytics transforms decision-making through detailed examples in four critical business areas. Each example illustrates the practical benefits of AI-driven insights, highlighting improvements in speed, accuracy, and operational effectiveness.

4.5.1 Sales Dashboards

Traditional sales reporting often relies on weekly or monthly reports that are already outdated when reviewed. Sales managers typically spend significant time compiling data from CRM systems, emails, and spreadsheets, and even then, trends and forecasts are difficult to detect. Management decisions are frequently reactive, based on historical results rather than proactive intelligence. AI-powered sales dashboards transform this process by providing continuous monitoring of performance metrics. Real-time performance monitoring enables sales teams to respond immediately to changes in pipeline health, rep performance, territory opportunities, and forecast accuracy.

For example, a mid-market software company with a sales team of 25 representatives faced challenges in pipeline visibility and forecast accuracy. The AI solution integrated CRM data, email communications, calendar activity, and customer support tickets. Predictive scoring models assessed deal characteristics, customer behavior, and rep activity to estimate close probabilities, while individual dashboards highlighted leading indicators of success. Market intelligence algorithms recommend territory optimizations and competitive strategies. Within six months, the company achieved a 35 percent improvement in forecast accuracy, a 25 percent increase in average deal size, a 40 percent reduction in sales cycle length, and a 20 percent improvement in rep productivity. Key dashboard components included a deal intelligence panel showing real-time pipeline value, predicted close rates, risk assessments, recommended actions, and competitive insights, as well as a performance optimization center tracking individual rep activity, leading indicators, coaching recommendations, and market opportunities.

4.5.2 Financial Anomaly Detection

Modern businesses process thousands of transactions daily across multiple systems, making manual oversight both impractical and prone to error. AI-powered financial monitoring provides multi-layer anomaly detection to identify potential fraud, errors, or operational issues. Transaction fraud can be detected in real time through pattern analysis and behavioral modeling, while expense anomalies and cash flow irregularities are identified through statistical outlier detection and predictive variance analysis. Revenue recognition is monitored using trend analysis and business rule validation on a weekly basis.

A regional retail chain operating 150 stores and processing $500 million annually implemented an AI anomaly detection system. Transaction monitoring analyzed all point-of-sale activity in real time, while vendor payments were reviewed automatically for duplicates, pricing anomalies, and unauthorized vendors. Inventory shrinkage was identified through AI analysis of stock movements, and automated validation ensured compliance in financial reporting. Within six months, the system prevented $75,000 in fraudulent credit card transactions, identified $150,000 in duplicate vendor payments, detected inventory issues at multiple locations, and avoided potential audit findings by catching revenue recognition errors. Advanced capabilities included behavioral analysis of employee spending, vendor relationships, and customer payment patterns, as well as cross-system correlation to link financial metrics with operational performance.

4.5.3 Marketing Optimization

Traditional marketing analytics often focus on post-campaign reporting, which limits the ability to respond quickly to changing market conditions. AI-powered marketing optimization enables real-time adjustments and predictive modeling of campaign performance. Campaign performance optimization includes automatic bid adjustments across channels, continuous audience refinement, creative testing with automated statistical validation, and multi-touch attribution modeling to guide budget allocation.

An e-commerce fashion retailer managing a $2 million annual marketing budget faced limited visibility into cross-channel performance. The AI system unified data across Google Ads, Facebook, Instagram, email, and influencer campaigns. Customer journey mapping allowed the system to track interactions across all touchpoints, while predictive models estimated customer lifetime value to optimize acquisition spending. Dynamic budget allocation automatically shifted resources to the highest-performing channels. As a result, return on ad spend improved by 45 percent, customer acquisition costs decreased by 30 percent, customer lifetime value increased by 60 percent, and campaign launch speed improved by 25 percent. AI capabilities included lookalike modeling and behavioral prediction for audience targeting, dynamic content optimization for personalized engagement, send-time prediction for timing optimization, and unified orchestration across channels to ensure a consistent brand experience.

4.5.4 Predictive Operations

Traditional operations management often reacts to issues after they occur, which can lead to costly downtime and reduced efficiency. Predictive operations use AI to anticipate problems and optimize performance proactively. Equipment and maintenance intelligence enables failure prediction based on sensor data, operating conditions, and maintenance history. Scheduling algorithms balance repair costs with production requirements, while predictive parts inventory management ensures that necessary components are available in advance. Performance optimization continuously adjusts operating parameters to maximize efficiency.

An automotive parts supplier operating a 24/7 manufacturing line implemented a predictive system integrating over 500 IoT sensors monitoring temperature, vibration, pressure, and production performance. AI models predicted equipment failures 48 to 72 hours in advance, and real-time analysis of production quality provided automatic adjustment recommendations. Demand forecasting integrated with supply chain management optimized production planning and supplier coordination. Operational improvements included a 65 percent reduction in unplanned downtime, a 40 percent decrease in maintenance costs, a 25 percent improvement in overall equipment effectiveness, and a 30 percent reduction in quality defects.

Cross-functional operations intelligence extended predictive insights to supply chain and workforce management. Multi-factor demand forecasting accounted for market trends, seasonality, and external events. Supplier performance and risk were continuously monitored, while dynamic logistics routing optimized delivery and inventory levels. Workforce analytics provided predictive staffing models, tracked individual and team performance, monitored safety, and generated personalized training recommendations. Successful implementation required clean and consistent data, real-time processing infrastructure, scalable architecture, robust security, executive sponsorship, cross-functional collaboration, user training, and a continuous improvement mindset.

4.6 Conclusion

AI-driven automated analytics is transforming the way businesses collect, analyze, and act on data. By progressing from descriptive analytics to predictive and prescriptive approaches, organizations gain a deeper understanding of their operations, anticipate future outcomes, and receive actionable recommendations that support confident decision-making. AI enhances these processes by identifying patterns that humans might overlook, processing large volumes of data in real time, and presenting insights with relevant business context.

Automation serves as an intelligence amplifier rather than a replacement for human judgment. Routine data processing and analysis are handled efficiently by AI, freeing decision-makers to focus on strategy, interpretation, and high-value actions. Well-designed alert systems function as a business nervous system, monitoring critical metrics continuously and directing attention only when intervention is needed. Intelligent prioritization reduces alert fatigue while ensuring timely response to urgent issues.

Real-world applications demonstrate that AI-powered analytics delivers measurable value across multiple functions. Sales dashboards improve forecast accuracy and pipeline management, financial monitoring detects anomalies and prevents losses, marketing optimization drives higher ROI, and predictive operations reduce downtime and enhance efficiency. The most successful implementations start with focused, high-impact use cases and scale systematically based on proven results.

Implementing an effective analytics strategy is a phased journey. Establishing foundational data connections and quality processes sets the stage for success, followed by deployment of predictive models and intelligent alerts. Ultimately, integrating prescriptive analytics and cross-functional intelligence achieves organization-wide adoption and continuous optimization.

Looking forward, emerging capabilities such as conversational analytics, autonomous systems, edge analytics, and explainable AI will make advanced insights more accessible, timely, and transparent. Building organizational competencies through business acumen, technical literacy, critical thinking, and change leadership—ensures that AI-driven analytics is not only implemented but fully leveraged to achieve business objectives.

Success depends on a combination of technical excellence, organizational readiness, and strong business alignment. High-quality, well-integrated data, scalable infrastructure, secure systems, and continuous optimization must be paired with leadership support, user training, and a culture of experimentation. When these elements come together, automated analytics evolves from a reporting tool into a strategic capability that drives smarter decisions, measurable outcomes, and sustained business advantage.

Chapter 5

AI-Enhanced Decision Making

5.1 Introduction

Imagine you're shopping online for a new laptop. As you browse, the website suggests products you might like, adjusts prices based on demand, and even predicts when items might go out of stock. Behind these seemingly simple features lies a complex world of AI-enhanced decision making that's transforming how businesses operate and how we interact with technology every day.

In our previous chapters, we explored how AI automates tasks, assists with daily work, integrates systems, and generates reports. Now we turn our attention to perhaps the most significant application of AI in business: helping make better decisions faster and more accurately than humans could alone.

Every day, businesses face thousands of decisions. Should we restock this product? Which customer should receive a discount offer? Is this loan application risky? Which job candidate should we interview? Traditionally, humans made all these choices using their experience, intuition, and available data. Today, AI systems can process vast amounts of information in seconds and suggest or even make many of these decisions automatically.

This chapter will help you understand when AI excels at decision making, when humans remain essential, and how the two work together most effectively. We'll explore real-world examples that demonstrate both the power and limitations of AI-enhanced decision making, always keeping in mind that technology serves people, not the other way around.

5.2 AI vs Human Decision Making

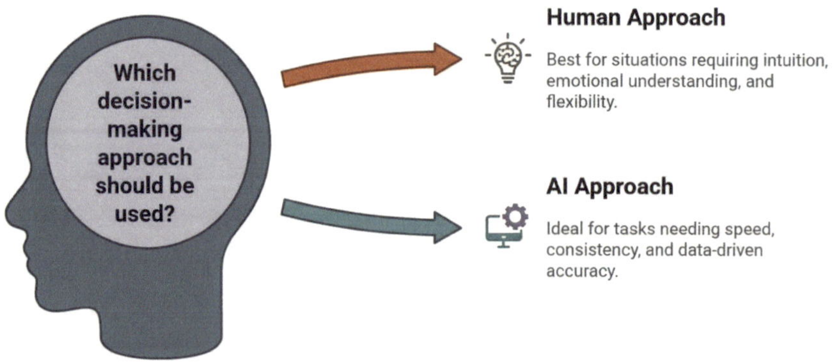

5.2.1 The Fundamental Difference

When you decide what to have for lunch, you consider many factors: your mood, the weather, what you ate yesterday, your budget, and perhaps what your friends are having. This decision feels effortless, but it involves complex reasoning that draws on memory, emotions, social context, and personal preferences.

AI systems approach decisions very differently. They excel at processing large amounts of structured data quickly and consistently, but they lack the intuitive understanding and contextual awareness that humans bring naturally to most situations. Understanding this fundamental difference helps us recognize where each approach works best.

Consider how Netflix recommends movies to you. The AI system analyzes your viewing history, the time of day, what similar users watched, current trending content, and dozens of other data points. It processes this information in milliseconds and suggests titles you're likely to enjoy. However, it cannot understand that you're feeling sad today and might want a comedy instead of the drama it would normally recommend based on your viewing patterns.

5.2.2 Where AI Excels in Decision Making

AI systems excel in decision-making when tasks involve analyzing large volumes of data, applying consistent rules, operating at high speed, or processing complex information. One area where AI performs particularly well is pattern recognition at scale. By identifying subtle patterns across massive datasets, AI can detect insights that humans might miss. For example, credit card companies use AI to uncover fraudulent transactions by analyzing spending patterns across millions of accounts. While a human analyst might spot obvious fraud, AI can identify sophisticated behaviors that indicate risk even when individual transactions appear normal.

AI also excels in applying rules consistently. Unlike humans, AI systems do not experience fatigue, distraction, or emotional bias. This allows them to evaluate structured decisions, such as loan applications, uniformly. Consistent rule application can reduce certain types of bias and ensure fair treatment across all cases.

Another strength of AI is speed and availability. AI systems can make decisions instantly and operate continuously, 24 hours a day, 365 days a year. Online retailers, for example, use AI to generate inventory alerts such as "Only three left in stock!" by continuously monitoring sales velocity, stock levels, and demand trends.

Finally, AI can process complex data. It can integrate numbers, text, images, and audio to inform decisions. Amazon's recommendation engine illustrates this capability by considering purchase history, browsing behavior, customer reviews, items in a shopping cart, and typical shopping times to suggest products a customer is likely to want. Across these capabilities, AI enhances decision-making by providing speed, accuracy, and insights that would be impractical or impossible for humans to achieve alone.

5.2.3 Where Humans Remain Essential

Despite AI's impressive capabilities, humans remain essential in decision-making areas where machines struggle. One such area is ethical and moral reasoning. Decisions that involve values, empathy, or fairness require human judgment. For example, when a hospital must allocate limited resources during a crisis, AI can provide data on patient conditions and resource availability but determining how to act fairly and ethically requires human deliberation.

Humans also excel in creative and strategic thinking. Developing a new marketing campaign or brand strategy requires cultural understanding, imagination, and strategic insight. While AI can analyze the performance of past campaigns, creating something truly innovative requires the human ability to make creative leaps and envision new possibilities.

Contextual understanding is another strength of humans. People can interpret subtleties that AI cannot, such as tone, intent, or underlying motivations. For instance, a customer service representative deciding how to handle a complaint considers the customer's history, tone, and the nuances of the situation to find the most effective resolution.

Humans are also critical when handling unprecedented situations. During events like the COVID-19 pandemic, businesses faced circumstances without historical precedent. AI trained on past patterns could not provide reliable guidance, and human leaders had to make decisions using judgment, analogies, and rapidly evolving information. Across these domains, human judgment complements AI, ensuring that decisions account for ethics, creativity, context, and uncertainty.

5.2.4 The Power of Human-AI Collaboration

The most effective decision-making occurs when humans and AI work together, combining their respective strengths. This collaboration allows each to focus on what they do best while complementing the other.

One form of collaboration is AI serving as an information provider. AI systems can gather and analyze large amounts of relevant data quickly. Humans interpret this information in context and make the final decisions. For example, a doctor might use an AI system to analyze medical images and identify potential issues, but the doctor makes the final diagnosis by considering the patient's full medical history, symptoms, and other factors that the AI cannot fully evaluate.

Another form is using AI for routine decisions while humans handle exceptions. Many businesses automatically process standard, low-risk decisions but flag unusual or high-risk cases for human review. Credit card companies often approve typical transactions automatically but send transactions with unusual patterns to human analysts for investigation.

A third form of collaboration involves humans setting parameters and AI executing within them. Humans define rules, goals, and priorities, and AI systems carry out decisions at scale based on those guidelines. For example, a retail manager may set overall pricing strategies and inventory targets, while AI systems adjust individual prices and restocking levels across thousands of products in real time.

5.3 Types of AI Decision-Making Systems

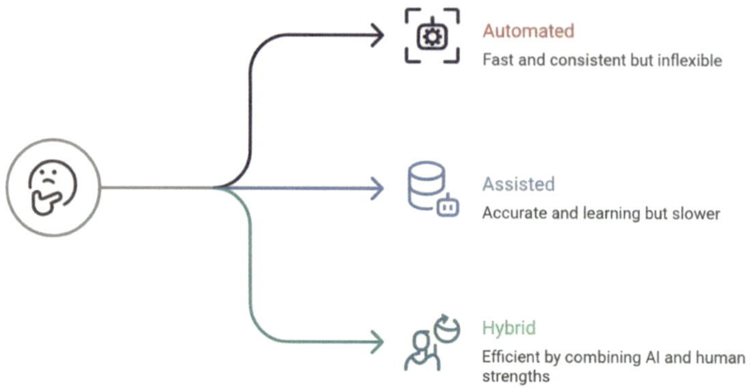

Understanding the different types of AI decision-making systems helps recognize them in action and evaluate their suitability for various situations. Most AI decision systems fall into three main categories, each with distinct characteristics and use cases.

Automated Decision Systems

Automated decision systems make choices without human intervention, following pre-programmed rules or learned patterns. They excel in high-volume, routine decisions where speed and consistency are more important than nuanced judgment.

These systems often operate using "if-then" logic or machine learning models trained on historical data. When specific conditions are met, the system automatically takes predetermined actions. Once set up, they operate independently, without needing human approval for each decision.

In dynamic pricing, airlines continuously adjust ticket prices based on demand, competitor pricing, time until departure, and historical patterns. When prices change within hours or minutes, automated decision systems are at work. In inventory management, Amazon's warehouses monitor sales velocity, seasonal trends, supplier lead times, and storage costs to determine when to reorder products, maintaining stock levels without human intervention.

Automated systems offer benefits such as speed, consistency, scalability, and cost efficiency. Their limitations include inflexibility in unusual situations, limited awareness of context, and the risk of repeating systematic errors.

AI-Assisted Decision Systems

AI-assisted systems provide analysis, recommendations, or predictions to support human decision-making. Humans remain in control, making the final choice, while AI enhances insight by identifying patterns or suggesting options.

In medical diagnosis, radiologists use AI to highlight areas in medical images that might indicate disease. The AI offers statistical assessments, but the radiologist integrates patient history, symptoms, and other factors to make the final diagnosis.

In financial investment, robo-advisors analyze an individual's financial situation, goals, and risk tolerance to recommend portfolios. They explain projected outcomes, but humans make the final decision and can override the AI's suggestions.

These systems offer benefits such as enhanced analysis, reduced bias, improved accuracy, and opportunities for humans to learn from AI insights. Limitations include the time required for human review, potential over-reliance on AI, and the complexity of interpreting AI outputs.

Hybrid Decision Systems

Hybrid systems combine automated and AI-assisted approaches, allowing AI to handle routine decisions while escalating complex or unusual situations to humans. These systems rely on confidence thresholds or rule-based triggers to determine when human intervention is necessary.

In loan approvals, straightforward applications that clearly meet criteria are automatically approved, and those that fail are automatically declined. Borderline cases are flagged for human review so decision-makers can consider contextual factors beyond AI capabilities.

Content moderation on social media is another example. AI automatically removes content that clearly violates policies and approves content that complies, while ambiguous cases are sent to human moderators who evaluate context, cultural nuances, and edge cases.

Hybrid systems offer benefits including efficiency, improved quality control, adaptability, and reduced risk of errors. They also have limitations: design and maintenance are more complex, setting appropriate thresholds can be challenging, and outcomes may vary depending on whether AI or humans make the final decision.

Choosing the Right System Type

The choice between automated, assisted, and hybrid systems depends on several factors:

Table 5.1: Factors Influencing Decision Automation Approaches

Factor	Automated	AI-assisted	Hybrid
Decision volume	Very high	Low to medium	High
Decision complexity	Low	High	Mixed
Speed requirements	Critical	Flexible	Important
Risk tolerance	Low risk	Variable	Medium risk
Human expertise available	Limited	High	Medium
Cost considerations	Low cost	Higher cost	Medium cost

5.4 Benefits and Risks of AI Decision Making

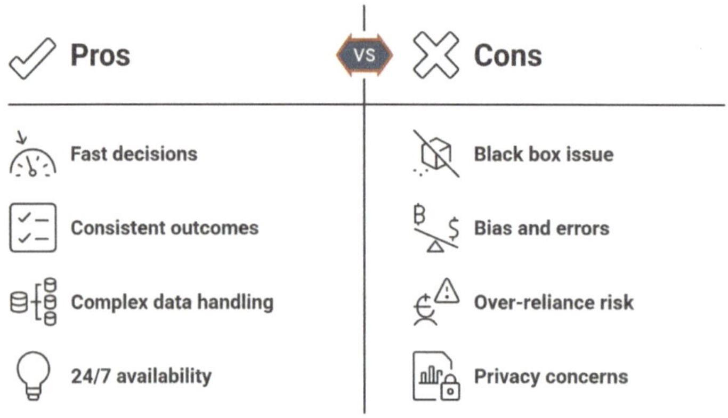

As AI decision-making systems become more prevalent in business and daily

life, understanding their benefits and risks becomes crucial for anyone working with data and technology. Like any powerful tool, AI decision making can create significant value when used appropriately, but it also introduces new challenges that require careful consideration.

5.4.1 Key Benefits of AI Decision Making

Improved Speed and Efficiency

One of the most immediate benefits of AI decision making is the dramatic improvement in speed. While a human analyst might take hours or days to review complex data and make a decision, AI systems can process the same information and reach conclusions in seconds or minutes.

Consider fraud detection in banking. Traditional methods required human analysts to review suspicious transactions manually, often taking hours or days to investigate each case. During this time, fraudulent transactions could continue, and legitimate customers might have their cards blocked unnecessarily. Modern AI systems can analyze transaction patterns in real-time, comparing each transaction against millions of historical patterns to detect fraud within milliseconds of the transaction occurring.

This speed improvement extends beyond individual decisions to organizational agility. Companies using AI decision systems can respond to market changes, customer behavior shifts, and operational issues much faster than competitors relying solely on human decision-making processes.

Enhanced Consistency and Reduced Human Bias

Humans are naturally inconsistent decision-makers. We're influenced by factors like time of day, recent experiences, mood, and unconscious biases. An HR manager reviewing resumes at 4 PM on Friday might make different decisions than the same manager reviewing identical resumes at 10 AM on Tuesday.

AI systems, when properly designed, apply the same criteria consistently to every decision. This consistency can significantly improve fairness in many contexts. For example, AI systems used in hiring can evaluate all candidates using identical criteria, potentially reducing bias based on factors like gender, race, or educational background that might unconsciously influence human recruiters.

However, it's important to note that AI systems can perpetuate or even amplify biases present in their training data. The consistency benefit only applies when the underlying system is designed fairly and trained on representative data.

Ability to Process Complex, Multi-Dimensional Data

Modern business decisions often involve analyzing multiple types of data simultaneously - numerical data, text, images, time series, and more. Humans excel at intuitive reasoning but struggle to process large amounts of complex data systematically.

AI systems can analyze thousands of variables simultaneously and identify subtle patterns that humans would never notice. Netflix's recommendation system considers your viewing history, the time you typically watch, what similar users enjoyed, current trending content, the devices you use, and even how you rate content to make personalized suggestions. No human analyst could process all these factors for millions of users simultaneously.

24/7 Availability and Scalability

AI decision systems never sleep, take breaks, or go on vacation. This constant availability is particularly valuable for global businesses operating across time zones or for applications requiring immediate responses.

Customer service chatbots exemplify this benefit. While human customer service representatives work specific hours, AI chatbots can handle customer inquiries around the clock. They can simultaneously assist thousands of customers, providing immediate responses to common questions and escalating complex issues to human agents when they become available.

5.4.2 Significant Risks and Challenges

Lack of Transparency and Explainability

Many AI systems, particularly those using deep learning, operate as "black boxes." They can make accurate predictions or decisions, but they cannot explain their reasoning in terms humans can easily understand. This lack of transparency creates several problems.

When a bank's AI system denies a loan application, the applicant deserves to understand why. However, if the AI system cannot provide clear, understandable reasons for its decision, this creates both legal and ethical problems. Regulations in many jurisdictions require that automated decisions affecting individuals be explainable.

The explainability challenge becomes even more critical in high-stakes decisions. If an AI system recommends a particular medical treatment or suggests a business strategy, decision-makers need to understand the reasoning to evaluate whether the recommendation makes sense in context.

Potential for Systematic Errors and Bias Amplification

While AI systems can reduce some types of human bias, they can also create new forms of bias or amplify existing ones. If an AI system is trained on historical data that reflects past discrimination, it may perpetuate those patterns.

Amazon discovered this problem when they developed an AI recruiting tool that showed bias against women. The system was trained on resumes submitted over a 10-year period, during which male candidates were more likely to be hired for technical roles. The AI learned to associate male-dominated language and experiences with successful candidates, effectively discriminating against female applicants [[1]].

When AI systems make errors, they often make them systematically and at scale. A flawed algorithm might make the same type of mistake thousands or millions of times before anyone notices the pattern.

Over-Reliance and Skill Atrophy

As AI systems become more capable, there's a risk that humans become overly dependent on them and lose the ability to make decisions independently. This over-reliance can be particularly dangerous when AI systems fail or encounter situations outside their training.

Pilots using advanced autopilot systems sometimes experience skill atrophy, becoming less capable of manually flying aircraft when automation fails. Similarly, business professionals who rely heavily on AI recommendations might lose their ability to analyze situations independently and make decisions when AI systems are unavailable or inappropriate.

Privacy and Ethical Concerns

AI decision systems often require access to large amounts of personal data to function effectively. This data collection and use raises significant privacy concerns, particularly when individuals are unaware of how their data influences decisions affecting them.

Insurance companies might use AI to analyze social media posts, purchasing patterns, and other personal data to assess risk and set premiums. While this might lead to more accurate pricing, it also raises questions about privacy and whether individuals should be penalized for legal activities that correlate with higher risk.

5.4.3 Risk Mitigation Strategies

Effective AI decision systems require robust risk mitigation strategies, beginning with human oversight and review processes. High-stakes or unusual decisions should include regular audits of AI decision patterns to identify potential biases or errors. Human review is important for decisions that exceed certain risk thresholds, and clear escalation procedures should be in place for situations the AI system cannot fully handle. Regular retraining of AI models using updated and diverse data helps ensure the system adapts to changing conditions and maintains reliability.

Transparency and explainability are also essential. Organizations should prioritize AI techniques that provide interpretable results whenever possible and develop clear explanations for how decisions are made. Individuals affected by AI-driven decisions should be provided with information about the factors influencing outcomes. Additionally, staff should be trained to understand AI system outputs and communicate the reasoning behind them effectively.

Continuous monitoring and improvement are critical to sustaining performance. Decision outcomes should be tracked to detect patterns of errors or bias, and training data must be updated regularly to reflect current conditions. AI systems should be tested against new scenarios and edge cases to ensure resilience, while human expertise remains essential to evaluate system performance and guide ongoing enhancements.

5.5 Framework for AI-Enhanced Decision Making

As AI becomes more integrated into business operations, organizations need systematic approaches for determining when and how to use AI in their decision-making processes. This section provides a practical framework that helps evaluate whether AI enhancement is appropriate for specific decisions and how to implement it effectively.

5.5.1 The DECIDE Framework for AI Integration

The DECIDE framework provides a structured approach for evaluating AI decision-making opportunities. Each letter represents a key consideration in determining whether and how to implement AI-enhanced decision making.

D – Define the Decision Context
The first step in the DECIDE framework is to define the decision context. This involves clearly understanding the decision you want to make by identifying which decisions are made repeatedly, who currently makes them, what information is used, how often the decision occurs, and the consequences of good versus poor outcomes. For example, a retail company might define inventory restocking decisions as determining when and how much inventory to order for each product at each store, made weekly by store managers using sales data, seasonal patterns, and intuition about local events.

E – Evaluate Data Availability and Quality
AI systems rely heavily on high-quality data to function effectively. Evaluating data availability involves assessing whether sufficient historical data exists, whether collection processes are reliable, whether the data covers the full range of situations the AI will encounter, and whether the data is accurate and clean. Using the inventory example, this would include historical sales data, seasonal patterns, promotional impacts, local event information, and supplier lead times. Incomplete or unreliable data can limit AI effectiveness unless data collection is improved first.

C – Consider the Complexity and Stakes
Before implementing AI, it is important to consider the complexity of the decision and the stakes involved. This means evaluating the number of variables

influencing the decision, whether subjective judgment or objective criteria are required, the cost of errors versus benefits of correct decisions, and whether mistakes can be easily corrected. Simple, objective decisions with clear criteria are often ideal candidates for AI, whereas complex, high-stakes, or subjective decisions may require human oversight even with AI assistance.

I – Identify the Appropriate AI Approach

Once the decision context and complexity are understood, the next step is identifying the appropriate AI approach. Automated systems are best suited for high-volume, routine decisions with clear criteria. AI-assisted systems provide insights and recommendations to support human judgment in complex scenarios. Hybrid systems combine these approaches, allowing AI to handle routine decisions while escalating ambiguous or high-stakes cases to humans. For example, in inventory management, standard products with predictable demand may be reordered automatically, while new or unusual items are flagged for human review.

D – Design Implementation and Oversight

Implementation planning ensures AI operates effectively while maintaining human control. This includes defining when AI can act independently versus when humans should intervene, establishing monitoring processes to track AI performance, creating feedback loops to continuously improve the system, and training staff to interact effectively with AI. Thoughtful design of oversight mechanisms helps prevent errors, manage risk, and ensure the AI system aligns with organizational goals.

E – Evaluate and Iterate

The final step is to continuously evaluate and iterate on the AI system. This involves comparing AI-enhanced decisions to previous human-only decisions, monitoring for unintended consequences or biases, collecting feedback from users and stakeholders, and updating the system based on new data and changing conditions. Iterative evaluation ensures that AI systems remain accurate, reliable, and aligned with organizational needs over time.

5.5.2 Decision Classification Matrix

To help apply the DECIDE framework systematically, use this classification matrix to categorize decisions based on two key dimensions: complexity and frequency.

Table 5.2: Frequency and Complexity Decision Matrix

Complexity	High frequency	Low frequency
Low complexity	Automate: Use fully automated AI systems for routine, rule-based decisions	Standardize: Create clear procedures, consider simple AI assistance
High complexity	Hybrid: Use AI for initial analysis, human review for final decisions	Human-led: Use AI for information gathering, human expertise for decisions

Examples by Category:

High Frequency, Low Complexity – Automate
Decisions that occur frequently but are relatively simple are ideal candidates for full automation. Examples include credit card fraud detection, basic customer service inquiries, inventory reordering for standard products, and email spam filtering. These tasks involve clear rules, high volumes, and minimal need for contextual judgment, allowing AI systems to act quickly and consistently without human intervention.

High Frequency, High Complexity – Hybrid
When decisions are both frequent and complex, hybrid systems are most effective. These systems allow AI to handle routine aspects while escalating ambiguous or high-stakes cases to humans. Examples include loan approval decisions, medical diagnosis support, investment recommendations, and content moderation on social platforms. The combination of automated efficiency and human oversight ensures accuracy, adaptability, and risk management.

Low Frequency, Low Complexity – Standardize
Decisions that happen infrequently and have low complexity are best addressed through standardized processes. Examples include employee expense

approvals, basic vendor selections, routine policy exceptions, and standard contract approvals. Standardization ensures consistency and reduces errors, while the low frequency means full automation may not be necessary.

Low Frequency, High Complexity – Human-Led

Infrequent decisions with high complexity require human judgment and expertise. Examples include strategic business decisions, crisis management responses, major investment decisions, and ethical policy development. These decisions often involve nuanced reasoning, ethical considerations, and contextual knowledge that AI cannot fully replicate, making human leadership essential.

5.5.3 Implementation Checklist

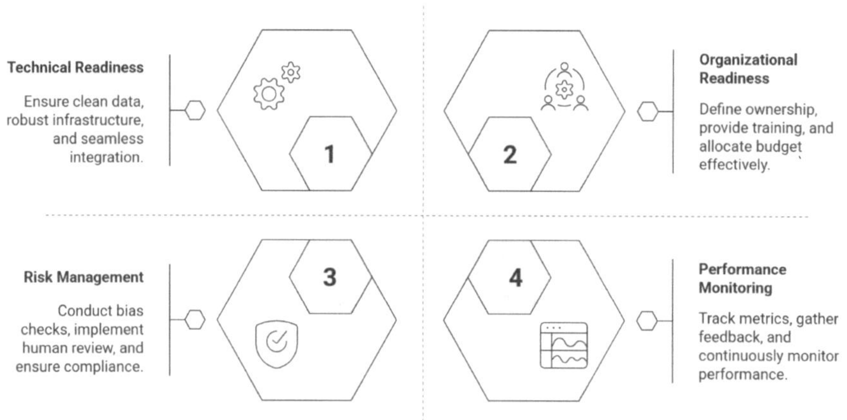

Before introducing AI into decision-making processes, it is important to step back and confirm that the organization is truly ready. This checklist highlights the core areas that should be in place before implementation begins.

Technical Readiness

AI systems rely on data and infrastructure to function properly. Organizations should ensure they have enough historical data, usually at least six to twelve months, and that this data is accurate, complete, and consistent. The existing technical infrastructure must be capable of supporting AI tools, and the AI system should be able to integrate smoothly with current software, databases, and workflows.

Organizational Readiness

Successful AI adoption depends as much on people as on technology. There should be clear ownership of the AI system, with accountability for its performance and outcomes. Staff need training to understand and work with AI recommendations, and a change management plan should guide the transition from current decision-making methods. Adequate budget support is also essential, not only for initial setup but for ongoing maintenance and improvements.

Risk Management

Every AI system introduces potential risks that must be managed carefully. Organizations should identify and address possible biases in training data and establish procedures for detecting and correcting errors. Clear rules should define when human oversight is required, especially for high-risk decisions. Compliance with legal, regulatory, and ethical standards must be built into the system from the start.

Performance Monitoring

Once an AI decision system is in place, continuous monitoring is critical. Success metrics such as accuracy, speed, cost savings, and user satisfaction should be clearly defined. Monitoring tools or dashboards should track system performance, and regular reviews should be scheduled to assess results. Feedback from users and stakeholders helps identify issues early and guides ongoing improvement.

5.5.4 Common Implementation Pitfalls to Avoid

One of the most common mistakes organizations make is starting too big. Teams are often tempted to apply AI to their most complex and high-stakes decisions right away, but this approach increases risk and frustration. A better strategy is to begin with simpler, lower-risk decisions, allowing the organization to build experience, trust, and confidence before expanding to more critical use cases.

Another frequent pitfall is ignoring change management. Implementing AI is not just a technical project; it is a human one. Employees need time, training, and reassurance to adapt to working alongside AI systems. Without clear communication and support, resistance can undermine even the most well-designed system.

Many organizations also expect perfection from AI systems. In reality, AI will make mistakes, especially in the early stages of deployment. Successful implementations plan for errors and focus on learning and improvement rather than assuming flawless performance from the start.

Neglecting data quality is another major risk. AI systems are only as good as the data they rely on, and poor or inconsistent data will lead to poor decisions no matter how advanced the algorithms are. Investing in clean, reliable data is a prerequisite for effective AI decision making.

Finally, organizations sometimes forget the human factors involved. AI systems are most effective when they complement human judgment rather than attempt to replace it entirely. Designing systems that support and enhance human decision-making leads to better outcomes than removing people from the process altogether.

5.6 Conclusion

As we conclude our exploration of AI-enhanced decision making, the future lies in partnerships between humans and AI, not in replacing human judgment. AI excels at processing vast amounts of data quickly, consistently, and at scale, while humans provide essential context, ethical reasoning, creativity, and the ability to handle unprecedented situations. The examples and frameworks discussed in this chapter illustrate current best practices, but the field continues to evolve rapidly as technology advances and organizations gain more experience with AI in real-world applications.

For future data professionals, the key takeaway is that value comes from understanding how to work effectively with AI systems. This includes evaluating AI recommendations in context, ensuring high-quality data for AI systems, applying ethical judgment, and guiding organizations through change as AI becomes a standard part of decision-making processes. The evolving landscape also includes more explainable and adaptable AI systems, as well as emerging regulations and governance frameworks that ensure AI is used responsibly and fairly.

Preparing for this AI-enhanced future requires comfort with AI assistance while maintaining critical thinking skills to evaluate and improve AI outputs. These systems are tools designed by humans to serve human purposes, and they work best when thoughtfully implemented with attention to their impact on individuals and society. The goal is not perfect AI decisions, but human-AI partnerships that achieve better outcomes than either could accomplish alone. By embracing these principles, professionals can navigate the increasingly AI-driven world of business and technology, and leverage AI's strengths while preserving the uniquely human capabilities that machines cannot replicate.

Chapter 6

Human Oversight in AI Systems

6.1 Introduction

Imagine you're using a navigation app to drive to an important meeting. The app suggests a route that takes you through a neighborhood you know is under construction. You can see the road work ahead, but your phone insists you should continue straight. What do you do? Most people would override the app's suggestion and take a different route, using their human judgment to make a better decision than the AI system.

This simple example illustrates a fundamental principle of AI systems: no matter how smart they become, humans must remain in control. While AI can process vast amounts of data and make rapid decisions, it cannot replace human judgment, especially when unexpected situations arise or when ethical considerations come into play.

In our previous chapters, we've explored how AI automates tasks, assists with decisions, and integrates into business processes. Now we turn to a critical aspect that ensures AI remains beneficial and safe: human oversight. This chapter will help you understand why human oversight is essential, how it works in practice, and how to design systems that keep humans appropriately involved in AI-driven processes.

Human oversight isn't about slowing down AI or limiting its capabilities. Instead, it's about creating partnerships between humans and AI that combine the best of both: AI's speed and consistency with human wisdom and accountability. When done well, human oversight makes AI systems more trustworthy, more effective, and more aligned with human values and goals.

6.2 Why Human Oversight is Essential

6.2.1 The Limitations of AI Decision-Making

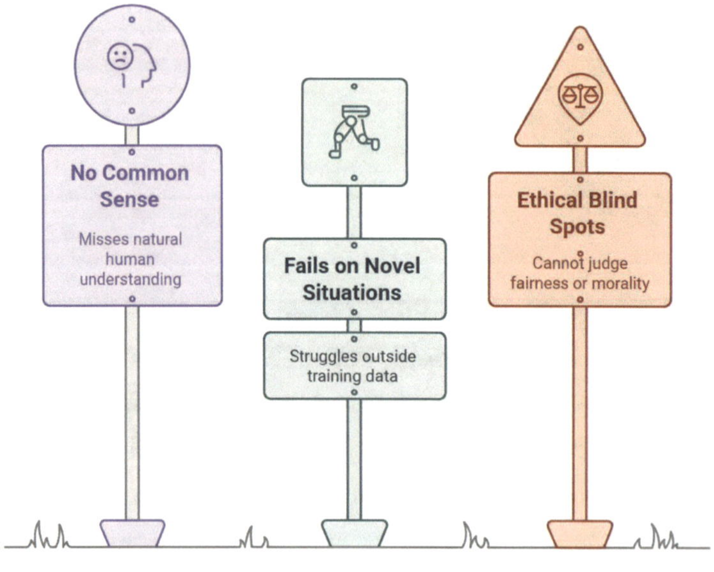

While AI systems excel in many areas, they have fundamental limitations that make human oversight necessary. Understanding these limitations helps us recognize when and why human involvement is crucial.

Lack of Common Sense and Context Understanding

AI systems process information very differently from humans. They can identify patterns in data and make predictions based on those patterns, but they often lack the common sense understanding that humans take for granted. Consider a simple example: an AI system managing office lighting might turn off lights in a conference room because it detects no movement for 10 minutes. However, it cannot understand that people in the room are sitting still during an important presentation and actually need the lights to stay on.

This limitation becomes more serious in complex business situations. An AI system analyzing customer complaints might flag a message as "urgent" because it contains words like "emergency" and "immediate," even if the customer is actually praising the company's emergency response service. A human reading the same message would immediately understand the positive context that the AI missed.

Inability to Handle Unprecedented Situations

AI systems learn from historical data and patterns. When they encounter situations that are significantly different from their training data, they can make poor decisions or fail entirely. The COVID-19 pandemic provided many examples of this limitation. AI systems trained on pre-pandemic data couldn't predict consumer behavior during lockdowns, supply chain disruptions, or the shift to remote work.

For instance, an AI system managing inventory for a restaurant chain might have learned that demand for takeout food is typically low on weekday afternoons. During the pandemic, when office workers started working from home, this pattern completely changed, but the AI system continued making decisions based on outdated patterns until humans intervened to retrain it.

Ethical Blind Spots

Perhaps most importantly, AI systems cannot make ethical judgments in the way humans can. They can be programmed to follow certain rules, but they cannot understand the spirit behind those rules or navigate complex ethical dilemmas that require weighing competing values.

Consider an AI system used in hiring that has been trained to identify successful employees based on historical data. If that historical data reflects past discrimination, the AI might perpetuate those biases without understanding that doing so is ethically wrong. The system might consistently rank candidates from certain backgrounds lower, not because they're less qualified, but because the historical data reflects past unfair hiring practices.

6.2.2 The Risks of Fully Automated Systems

When AI systems operate without appropriate human oversight, several serious risks emerge that can harm individuals, organizations, and society.

Systematic Errors at Scale

One of the most dangerous aspects of unsupervised AI systems is their ability to make the same mistake repeatedly and at massive scale. Unlike human errors, which tend to be random and limited in scope, AI errors are often systematic and can affect thousands or millions of decisions before anyone notices the problem.

A real-world example occurred when an AI system used by a major retailer incorrectly learned to associate certain zip codes with higher return rates. The system began automatically declining orders from these areas, effectively discriminating against entire communities. Because the system processed thousands of orders daily, this error affected many customers before human oversight identified and corrected the problem.

Loss of Human Skills and Judgment

When humans become overly dependent on AI systems, they can lose the skills and judgment needed to make decisions independently. This phenomenon, sometimes called "automation bias," occurs when people defer to AI recommendations even when their own knowledge suggests a different course of action.

Pilots provide a well-documented example of this risk. As aircraft autopilot systems became more sophisticated, some pilots became less skilled at manual flying. In emergency situations where autopilot systems failed or behaved unexpectedly, pilots sometimes struggled to take control effectively. This led to new training requirements that ensure pilots maintain their manual flying skills even as they work with advanced automated systems.

Accountability Gaps

Without proper human oversight, it becomes difficult to assign responsibility when AI systems make harmful decisions. If an AI system denies someone a loan, approves a risky investment, or misdiagnoses a medical condition, who is accountable for the consequences? Clear human oversight ensures that there are always identifiable people responsible for AI decisions and their outcomes.

6.2.3 The Benefits of Appropriate Human Oversight

When implemented thoughtfully, human oversight enhances rather than hinders AI system performance while ensuring safety and accountability.

Enhanced Decision Quality

Human oversight often improves the quality of AI decisions by catching errors, providing context, and handling edge cases that AI systems struggle with. Humans can recognize when an AI recommendation doesn't make sense in the broader context, even if the AI's analysis appears technically correct.

For example, an AI system analyzing social media sentiment might classify posts about a company's "killer app" as negative because it focuses on the word "killer." A human reviewer would immediately understand that this is positive slang and correct the classification. This human input not only fixes the immediate error but can also help improve the AI system's future performance.

Maintained Trust and Acceptance

People are more likely to trust and accept AI systems when they know humans remain involved in important decisions. This trust is crucial for the successful adoption of AI technologies. When people understand that they can appeal AI decisions to humans or that humans review AI recommendations, they're more comfortable using these systems.

Healthcare provides a clear example of this principle. Patients are generally more accepting of AI-assisted diagnosis when they know a human doctor reviews and confirms the AI's analysis. The combination of AI efficiency and human oversight creates a system that patients trust more than either pure AI or pure human analysis alone.

Continuous Learning and Improvement

Human oversight creates feedback loops that help AI systems improve over time. When humans correct AI errors or override AI decisions, this information can be used to retrain and improve the AI models. Without human oversight, AI systems miss these learning opportunities and may continue making the same mistakes indefinitely.

6.3 Models of Human-AI Collaboration

Understanding different models of human-AI collaboration helps organizations choose the right approach for their specific needs and risk tolerance. Each model represents a different balance between AI efficiency and human control, with distinct advantages and appropriate use cases.

6.3.1 Human-in-the-Loop (HITL) Model

The Human-in-the-Loop (HITL) model is an AI decision-making approach in which humans remain directly involved in every decision. In this model, the AI system analyzes data, identifies patterns, and generates recommendations, but it does not act independently. A human decision-maker reviews the AI's output and makes the final determination. HITL is most appropriate when decisions are high-stakes, ethically sensitive, or require professional judgment that extends beyond what data alone can capture.

In practice, HITL systems function as decision-support tools rather than decision-makers. The AI processes large volumes of information and presents its findings along with confidence levels or explanations, allowing the human to evaluate the recommendation in context. The human can accept the AI's suggestion, modify it, or reject it entirely. This structure allows organizations to benefit from AI's speed and analytical power while preserving human oversight, responsibility, and contextual understanding.

A common and well-suited use case for the HITL model is medical imaging. In radiology, AI systems scan X-rays, CT scans, or MRIs and highlight areas that may indicate abnormalities such as tumors or fractures. The radiologist then reviews these suggestions, considers the patient's medical history and symptoms, and makes the final diagnosis. This approach improves efficiency and accuracy while ensuring that critical medical decisions remain under human control, making HITL ideal for environments where errors carry serious consequences.

6.3.2 Human-on-the-Loop (HOTL) Model

The Human-on-the-Loop (HOTL) model allows AI systems to make decisions automatically while humans remain in a supervisory role. In this approach, AI handles routine, high-volume decisions on its own, and humans monitor overall system behavior rather than reviewing every individual decision. HOTL is designed to balance efficiency and oversight, ensuring that AI operates at scale while humans retain the ability to intervene when something goes wrong or falls outside expected patterns.

In practice, HOTL systems rely on predefined rules, confidence thresholds, and monitoring tools. The AI executes decisions in real time, while humans observe performance through dashboards, alerts, and periodic reviews. When the system detects uncertainty, abnormal behavior, or potential risk, it flags the situation for human attention. This allows humans to step in only when necessary, focusing their expertise on exceptions rather than routine cases.

A clear use case for the HOTL model is credit card fraud detection. AI systems evaluate every transaction instantly, approving routine purchases and blocking those that clearly match fraud patterns. When activity looks unusual—such as a sudden overseas purchase or an unusually large charge—the system alerts human analysts or the customer for confirmation. This model enables rapid, round-the-clock protection while preserving human judgment for ambiguous or high-risk situations where automated decisions alone may not be sufficient.

6.3.3 Human-out-of-the-Loop (HOOTL) Model

The Human-out-of-the-Loop (HOOTL) model represents fully automated decision making, where AI systems operate independently with no real-time human involvement. Humans contribute during system design, training, and maintenance, but once deployed, the AI makes decisions on its own. This model prioritizes speed, consistency, and scale, and is appropriate only for well-defined, low-risk decisions where outcomes are reversible or have limited impact.

In practice, HOOTL systems rely entirely on predefined logic and learned patterns to act autonomously. Because there is no opportunity for immediate human intervention, these systems must be carefully tested and tightly scoped. Email spam filtering is a common example. AI systems automatically classify millions of emails each day as spam or legitimate by analyzing sender reputation, message content, and embedded links. While users can correct mistakes after the fact, the initial decision is made entirely by the AI to keep communication flowing efficiently.

Another use case is high-frequency trading, where AI systems execute trades in microseconds based on market data and algorithmic strategies. The speed of these decisions makes human involvement impossible in real time, so oversight occurs only through system design and post-hoc monitoring. While HOOTL systems deliver maximum efficiency and scalability, they also carry higher risk, since errors can propagate rapidly and unexpected situations cannot be addressed without halting or redesigning the system.

6.3.4 Choosing the Right Collaboration Model

The choice between HITL, HOTL, and HOOTL depends on several key factors that organizations must carefully consider:

Table 6.1: Human-in-the-Loop Decision Framework

Factor	HITL	HOTL	HOOTL
Decision stakes	High (life, safety, major financial)	Medium (moderate financial, operational)	Low (routine, easily reversible)
Volume	Low to medium	High	Very high
Speed requirements	Flexible	Important	Critical
Predictability	Low (many exceptions)	Medium (some exceptions)	High (routine patterns)
Regulatory requirements	Strict oversight required	Moderate oversight	Minimal oversight
Error tolerance	Very low	Low to medium	Medium to high

6.4 Designing Systems That Request Human Input Effectively

Designing AI systems that can recognize their own limitations is essential for responsible decision making. The goal is not to eliminate human involvement, but to ensure that human input is requested precisely when AI confidence is low or when situations fall outside normal patterns. Well-designed intervention systems preserve efficiency while protecting against errors, bias, and unexpected consequences.

Recognizing Low Confidence and Unusual Situations

Effective human-intervention design begins with enabling AI systems to detect uncertainty. Modern AI systems can estimate how confident they are in a decision by analyzing how closely new inputs match patterns seen during training. When inputs are familiar and data quality is high, confidence tends to be strong. When data is incomplete, contradictory, or unfamiliar, confidence decreases and human review becomes necessary.

Confidence scores must be interpreted carefully. High confidence does not guarantee correctness, particularly if training data contains bias or gaps. Low confidence does not always indicate failure, but it does signal that the situation deserves closer human attention. Systems should therefore treat confidence as a trigger for review rather than as proof of accuracy.

In addition to confidence scores, systems should monitor unusual patterns. These include inputs that differ significantly from historical data, combinations of signals that rarely occur together, sudden shifts in decision behavior, or external changes such as new regulations or market disruptions. When these conditions appear, the system should request human input even if numerical confidence appears high.

Using Confidence Thresholds to Trigger Human Review

Confidence thresholds translate uncertainty into action. Designers must determine when AI decisions are allowed to proceed automatically and when they should pause for human input. These thresholds should be based on the consequences of errors rather than on technical convenience.

For example, a loan approval system might allow fully automated decisions when confidence is very high and the financial risk is low. Applications with mixed signals, such as strong credit history but irregular income, should trigger human review. Very low-confidence cases should be escalated immediately, ensuring that potentially unfair or harmful decisions are never made automatically.

Thresholds are not static. They should be reviewed regularly and adjusted as the system learns, business conditions change, or risk tolerance evolves.

Designing Exception Handling for Unusual Cases

Human input is most valuable when AI encounters situations it was not designed to resolve alone. Exception handling mechanisms define how systems respond when confidence is low or when rules conflict.

One common exception involves data quality. If input data is missing, inconsistent, or contradictory, the system should avoid making assumptions and instead request human clarification. Another exception occurs when AI recommendations conflict with established business rules. In such cases, human judgment is needed to determine whether a rule should be enforced or intentionally overridden.

Regulatory and compliance concerns are another critical trigger for human involvement. When decisions could have legal or ethical implications, AI systems should defer to trained professionals who understand regulatory context and organizational responsibility.

Escalation Paths That Match Human Expertise

Requesting human input is only effective if the right person receives the request. Well-designed systems use tiered escalation so that decisions are reviewed by humans with appropriate authority and expertise. Routine exceptions can be handled by front-line staff, while complex, high-impact, or policy-related issues are escalated to specialists or managers.

Clear escalation paths reduce delays and prevent decision bottlenecks. They also ensure that humans are not overwhelmed with cases that fall outside their scope of responsibility.

Designing Alerts Humans Can Act On

Alerts should help humans make decisions, not distract or confuse them. Each request for human input should clearly explain what decision is required, why the AI could not proceed confidently, and how urgent the situation is. Providing relevant context, confidence explanations, and suggested actions allows humans to respond efficiently without redoing the AI's work from scratch.

To prevent alert fatigue, systems should prioritize alerts based on risk and urgency, group low-priority cases when possible, and continuously refine thresholds using feedback from human reviewers. If humans frequently confirm AI decisions, thresholds may be adjusted to reduce unnecessary interruptions. If humans frequently override AI decisions, the system may require retraining or tighter controls.

Supporting Safe and Accountable Human Overrides

Human input must include the ability to override AI decisions when necessary. Overrides should be easy to perform, clearly documented, and auditable. Each override should record who made the decision, what was changed, when it occurred, and why human judgment differed from the AI's recommendation.

These records serve two purposes. They preserve accountability for high-stakes decisions, and they provide valuable feedback that can improve future AI performance. Over time, well-designed override systems strengthen both human trust and system reliability.

Designing for Trust and Reliability

Systems that request human input effectively do more than manage risk. They build trust. When humans understand why AI systems ask for help and feel confident in their ability to intervene meaningfully, collaboration improves. AI becomes a partner rather than a black box, and decision quality improves across the organization.

Designing for low confidence and unusual situations is not a technical afterthought. It is a core requirement for responsible AI integration and a defining skill for professionals building AI-enhanced decision systems.

Accountability, Audit Trails, and Human Control

Implementing AI systems does not remove human responsibility for decisions. Instead, accountability must be deliberately designed into AI systems through audit trails, override capabilities, and clear responsibility structures. These mechanisms ensure that humans remain in control, decisions can be reviewed and corrected, and organizations can explain and defend AI-supported actions.

Audit Trails as the Foundation of Accountability

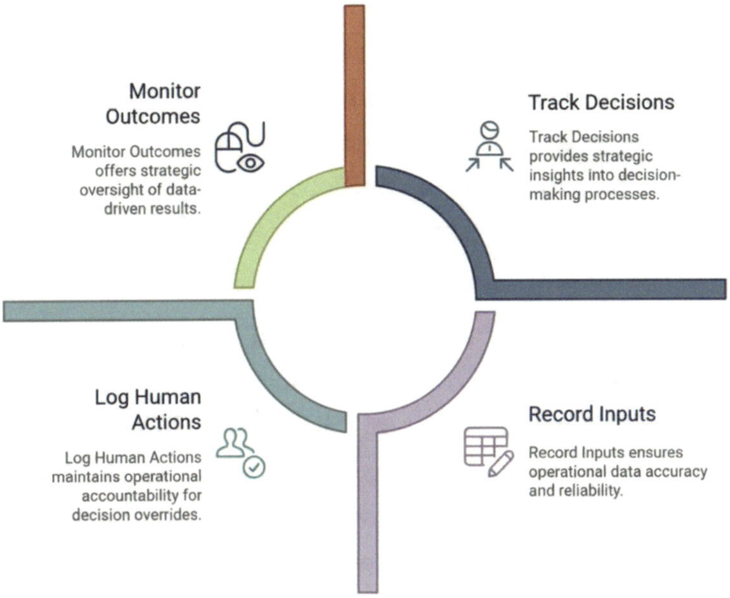

Audit trails are essential for maintaining accountability in AI-driven decision systems. They function as a detailed record of what decisions were made, what information was used, and how the system arrived at its conclusions. Without audit trails, organizations cannot investigate errors, respond to complaints, or demonstrate compliance with legal and ethical standards.

A well-designed audit trail records the input data used for each decision, including data sources, timestamps, and indicators of data quality. This makes it possible to determine whether a flawed outcome resulted from incomplete or incorrect data rather than a failure of the AI model itself. Audit trails should also capture decision-related metadata, such as confidence scores, thresholds applied, and key factors that influenced the system's recommendation. While complex models may not be fully explainable, recording these signals provides enough transparency for meaningful oversight.

Human involvement must also be logged. Any review, approval, modification, or override of an AI decision should be documented with the identity of the reviewer, the time of the intervention, and the reason for the action. Finally, audit systems should track outcomes over time, allowing organizations to evaluate whether AI-supported decisions actually led to successful or harmful results. This outcome tracking supports continuous improvement and long-term accountability.

Override Capabilities and Human Control

Audit trails alone are not sufficient if humans cannot intervene when necessary. AI systems must include explicit override mechanisms that allow authorized individuals to stop, modify, or reverse AI decisions. These overrides ensure that AI recommendations remain advisory rather than absolute, particularly in high-stakes or ambiguous situations.

Override capabilities should be easy to use but carefully controlled. Not every user should have the authority to override AI decisions, and override actions should always be recorded in the audit trail. Requiring a brief justification for overrides strengthens accountability and provides valuable feedback for improving system design. Patterns of frequent overrides may indicate bias, data problems, or overly aggressive automation thresholds that need correction.

Importantly, override systems reinforce human responsibility rather than weakening it. When humans know they retain decision authority, they are more likely to engage critically with AI recommendations instead of deferring blindly to automated outputs.

Maintaining Clear Human Accountability

For accountability measures to be effective, responsibility must be clearly assigned to identifiable people. Every AI system should have defined human owners who are accountable for its behavior and impact. Senior system owners are responsible for approving AI use, defining acceptable risk, and responding to serious failures. Technical operators manage system performance, data quality, and updates. Decision reviewers are accountable for individual outcomes in systems that require human approval, while end users are responsible for appropriate use and escalation of concerns.

Clear accountability structures prevent organizations from shifting blame to "the algorithm" when problems occur. Instead, they ensure that AI-supported decisions remain human decisions with traceable responsibility.

Accountability in Practice: Medical AI Example

In a medical diagnostic system, accountability is enforced through detailed audit trails and override authority. For each patient case, the system records symptoms, test results, and imaging data used in the analysis, along with diagnostic confidence scores and influencing factors. Physician interactions are logged, including whether the doctor accepted, modified, or rejected the AI recommendation. Treatment outcomes are tracked over time, linking decisions to real-world results.

If a diagnostic error occurs, clinicians and administrators can trace exactly how the decision was made, who reviewed it, and whether human intervention occurred. This transparency allows hospitals to improve patient safety, refine AI tools, and reinforce professional accountability.

Governance Structures That Support Accountability

Organizations must support technical accountability measures with governance structures that define oversight and escalation processes. Governance frameworks establish how audit data is reviewed, how override patterns are evaluated, and how responsibility is enforced when systems fail.

Regular performance reviews ensure audit data is examined rather than merely stored. Incident response procedures define how organizations react when AI causes harm, including immediate containment, investigation, and corrective action. Governance bodies also determine when AI systems should be paused, retrained, or withdrawn entirely.

These structures ensure that accountability mechanisms remain active and effective throughout the system's lifecycle, not just at deployment.

Compliance and Regulatory Alignment

Accountability measures also play a critical role in meeting regulatory requirements. Many laws governing data privacy, discrimination, and automated decision-making require organizations to explain decisions, document processes, and provide avenues for human review. Audit trails, override logs, and clear responsibility chains provide the evidence needed to demonstrate compliance.

Organizations that embed accountability into system design are better prepared to adapt to evolving regulations, respond to audits, and maintain public trust. Treating accountability as a core system feature rather than an afterthought reduces legal risk and strengthens ethical decision-making.

Accountability as a Design Requirement

Implementing audit trails and override capabilities is not merely a technical task. It is a design commitment to maintaining human control in AI-supported environments. Systems that record decisions, allow human intervention, and assign responsibility clearly are safer, more trustworthy, and more sustainable over time.

By preserving transparency and human authority, accountability measures ensure that AI enhances decision-making without undermining, a critical requirement for any organization using AI in real-world operations.

6.5 Conclusion

This chapter has shown that effective AI systems are not defined by how much they automate, but by how well they integrate human judgment, accountability, and oversight. Human-centered AI design does not weaken AI's capabilities; it strengthens them by ensuring that decisions remain aligned with human values, ethical standards, and real-world context. Trust emerges when AI systems are transparent, appropriately supervised, and clearly designed to support—not replace—human decision making.

As AI becomes more embedded in everyday business and organizational processes, the nature of human oversight will continue to evolve. AI systems may become better at recognizing uncertainty and signaling when human input is needed, but humans will remain ultimately responsible for high-stakes, ethical, and unprecedented decisions. Designing systems that balance efficiency with meaningful human control is therefore not optional—it is essential.

For future data and analytics professionals, the key takeaway is clear: success with AI depends as much on judgment, ethics, and communication as it does on technical skill. Those who understand how to evaluate AI outputs, question recommendations, and maintain accountability will play a critical role in shaping responsible AI use. The goal is not perfect automation, but better decisions made through thoughtful human–AI partnerships that preserve trust, agency, and responsibility in an increasingly AI-enabled world.

Chapter 7

AI Quality Control and System Reliability

7.1 Introduction

Imagine you're using your favorite music streaming app to discover new songs. You click on a playlist the app recommended, but instead of music you'd enjoy, it's filled with songs in a language you don't speak and a genre you dislike. You try again, but the same thing happens. Frustrated, you switch to a different app. This scenario shows why quality control matters—when AI systems don't work properly, people stop using them.

In our previous chapters, we've learned how AI systems make decisions, work with humans, and integrate into businesses. Now we need to answer an important question: How do we make sure these AI systems actually work well? Quality control and system reliability are about ensuring AI systems do what they're supposed to do, when they're supposed to do it.

Think about the AI systems you use every day. When you search for something online, you expect relevant results. When your bank's app checks for fraud, you want it to catch real problems without blocking your legitimate purchases. When a navigation app gives you directions, you need them to be accurate and timely. All of these expectations depend on quality control—the processes that ensure AI systems work correctly.

This chapter will teach you the basics of ensuring AI systems work reliably. You'll learn simple ways to measure how well AI systems perform, common problems to watch out for, and practical techniques for monitoring AI systems to catch issues early.

7.2 Measuring AI System Performance

Before improving an AI system, you need to know how well it is performing. Measuring performance means tracking simple metrics that indicate whether the system is making correct decisions and whether people find it useful.

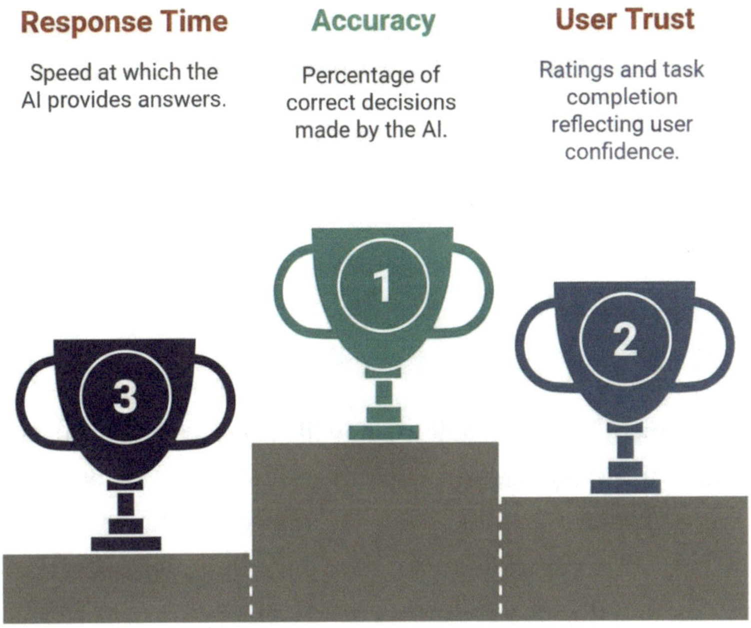

7.2.1 Accuracy: How Often the AI Is Correct

Accuracy measures the percentage of correct decisions the AI makes. For example, if a spam filter correctly classifies 90 out of 100 emails, its accuracy is 90%. Accuracy shows reliability, but high accuracy alone does not guarantee the system meets user needs.

A social media platform might measure accuracy in a photo-tagging system by comparing the number of correctly tagged faces to the total processed. If 850 of 1,000 photos are correctly tagged, the system's accuracy is 85%. This simple metric helps identify areas for improvement and track performance over time.

7.2.2 User Satisfaction: Whether People Trust the AI

Even a highly accurate system can fail if users dislike it or avoid it. User satisfaction measures whether people find the AI helpful, intuitive, and reliable. This can be tracked through ratings, usage patterns, or customer complaints. For example, an online store's chatbot might be correct in 75% of responses, but if customers rate it 4.2 out of 5 stars and 60% complete their interactions without human help, it shows the system is effective in practice.

7.2.3 Response Time: How Fast the AI Responds

Speed matters for many AI applications, especially real-time systems. Measuring average response time helps determine whether the system meets user expectations. For instance, the same chatbot responding within two seconds ensures a smooth experience while maintaining accuracy and satisfaction.

7.2.4 Setting Goals and Tracking Performance

Once metrics are defined, it's important to set realistic performance goals. These goals can be based on human performance, previous systems, or competitor benchmarks. For example, a hospital using AI to assist with pneumonia diagnosis might aim for 90% accuracy (compared to 85% for junior doctors), results within five minutes, and doctor satisfaction of 4+ stars.

AI systems should be monitored regularly because performance can change due to new data patterns, system updates, or seasonal effects. Simple daily or weekly tracking can detect declines, like a weather prediction system whose accuracy drops from 88% to 79% over a week, signaling a need for investigation.

7.3 Common AI System Problems

Understanding how AI systems fail is essential for spotting problems early and preventing serious consequences. Most failures can be traced to data issues, system design flaws, or integration problems. By recognizing typical failure patterns and early warning signs, you can intervene before issues escalate.

7.3.1 Data-Related Problems

Many AI failures start with data. Since AI systems learn patterns from historical information, poor-quality or outdated data often leads to unreliable decisions. Outdated training data is a common issue. For example, a job recommendation system trained on 2019 data continued to suggest office jobs and travel positions in 2021, failing to account for pandemic-related changes in remote work and industry demand. Similarly, poor data quality—such as missing fields, incorrect entries, inconsistent formats, or duplicate records—can disrupt decision-making. A retail store's inventory AI struggled when barcode scanners missed sales, returned items weren't updated promptly, and seasonal holiday data was absent, causing poor restocking choices.

Bias or unrepresentative data is another frequent problem. Early voice recognition systems often performed poorly for users with accents because the training data primarily included native English speakers, and testing didn't cover diverse speech patterns. These examples highlight that even sophisticated AI can fail if the underlying data is flawed or incomplete.

7.3.2 System Design Problems

Even with high-quality data, AI systems can fail due to design issues or inappropriate application. AI is not suitable for every task—especially those requiring human judgment, creativity, ethics, or emotional intelligence. For instance, companies that replaced all human customer service with chatbots found users frustrated. The AI could not handle complex problems, emotional situations, or exceptions to policy, showing that system design must match the task's requirements.

7.3.3 Integration and Technical Problems

AI systems rarely operate in isolation. Failures can occur when AI interacts poorly with databases, external services, or other software components. Integration issues—such as lost database connections, API failures, format mismatches, or delayed information—can disrupt performance. For example, a ride-sharing app experienced system failures when its AI could not access traffic data, verify payments, communicate with drivers, or receive accurate GPS information.

These issues show that technical reliability and system integration are as important as the AI model itself.

7.3.4 Early Warning Signs

Recognizing early warning signs allows organizations to address problems before they become critical. Gradual declines in performance metrics, such as slowly decreasing accuracy, longer response times, rising user complaints, or changing usage patterns, often indicate underlying issues. Changes in user behavior also signal problems: decreased usage, more requests for human assistance, negative feedback, or workaround behaviors can reveal that the AI system is not meeting expectations. By monitoring these indicators, teams can intervene proactively, improve system performance, and maintain user trust.

7.4 Basic Testing and Monitoring Strategies

Testing and monitoring are essential for maintaining AI system quality. Testing allows you to evaluate different approaches and determine which works best, while monitoring ensures that problems are identified and addressed promptly.

7.4.1 A/B Testing for AI Systems

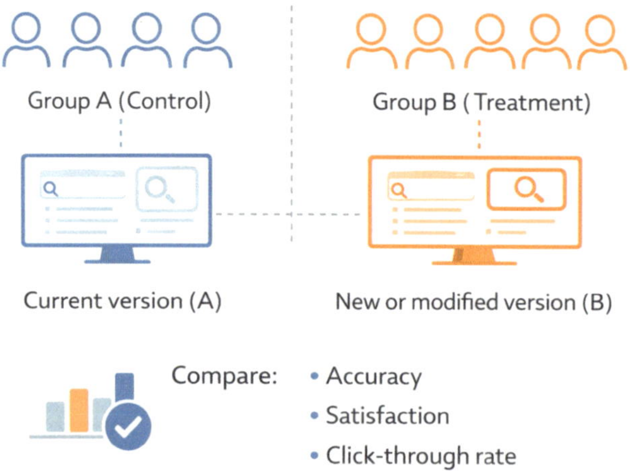

A/B testing is a simple and effective method for comparing two versions of an AI system. In this approach, users are randomly divided into two groups: one group experiences the current version of the system (the control), and the other group uses a new or modified version (the treatment). By comparing the performance of the two groups based on predefined metrics, organizations can determine which version provides better results.

For example, a search engine might test a new ranking algorithm using A/B testing. Group A receives results from the current algorithm, while Group B sees results from the new version. After two weeks, metrics like click-through rate and user satisfaction are compared. If Group B shows higher engagement and satisfaction, the new algorithm is adopted. This method ensures that improvements are validated with real user data before full deployment.

Setting up an A/B test involves several key steps. First, select the specific feature or change to test, ensuring it is significant enough to matter. Next, define success metrics that reflect real user value, such as accuracy, satisfaction, or task completion rates. Then, determine an appropriate test size and duration to achieve reliable results and account for daily or weekly usage patterns. Finally, randomly assign users to groups and ensure they consistently experience the same version throughout the test.

7.4.2 Monitoring AI Performance

Beyond testing new approaches, continuous monitoring is critical to maintain AI system effectiveness. Monitoring involves tracking performance metrics such as accuracy, error rates, response time, and usage volume. It also includes user experience indicators like satisfaction ratings, task completion rates, return usage, and support requests.

For instance, a translation app might monitor accuracy by measuring user corrections, track response time in seconds, record daily active users, and collect satisfaction ratings. Monitoring these metrics daily helps the team spot declining performance trends before they become serious problems.

7.4.3 Alerts and Dashboards

To act quickly on performance issues, AI systems should include alerts and dashboards. Alerts notify teams when metrics fall below acceptable thresholds or when trends indicate deteriorating performance. Types of alerts can include threshold alerts, trend alerts, and comparison alerts. For example, an alert might trigger if user satisfaction drops below 3.5 stars, or if accuracy falls under 80%.

Dashboards provide a visual overview of AI system performance, making trends and issues easy to spot. Effective dashboards highlight key metrics, show performance trends over time, and provide actionable insights. A customer service chatbot dashboard, for instance, could display current system status, response time, active conversations, recent alerts, and historical trends in accuracy and user satisfaction. Well-designed dashboards allow teams to monitor AI health efficiently and intervene when necessary.

7.5 Building Reliable AI Monitoring Systems

Creating reliable AI systems requires not just good design, but also ongoing monitoring and the ability to respond quickly when problems arise. Effective monitoring ensures that AI continues to perform as intended and allows teams to address issues before they impact users.

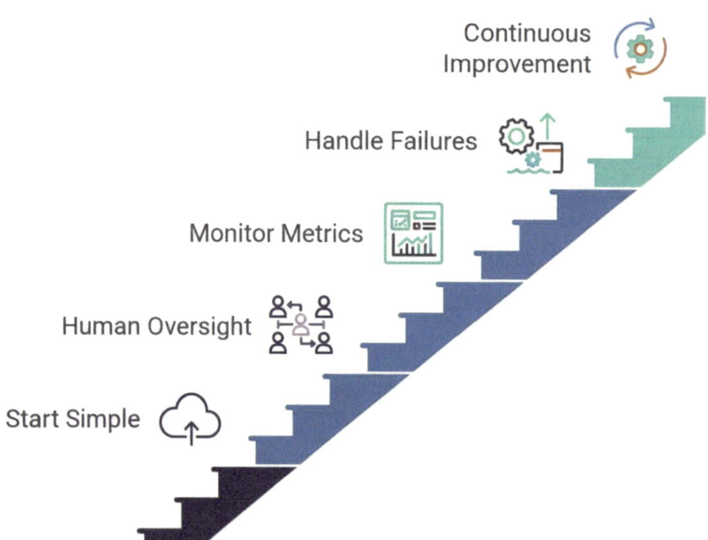

Start Simple and Build Gradually

Reliable AI begins with simple, understandable designs. Starting with basic algorithms makes it easier to track performance, identify errors, and debug problems. As confidence grows, complexity can be added incrementally, testing each addition carefully and maintaining fallback options. For example, an email spam detection system might begin with keyword filtering, then add sender reputation checks, followed by machine learning for content analysis, and finally advanced AI for sophisticated detection. If advanced AI fails, simpler methods continue to protect users.

Include Human Oversight

Even with automated systems, human oversight is essential. Monitoring systems should provide clear explanations for AI decisions and allow humans to intervene or override outputs when necessary. Regular review of AI performance, along with escalation procedures for unusual or high-stakes situations, ensures that humans remain in control and can correct errors promptly.

Monitoring Metrics and Alerts

Simple monitoring systems track key performance metrics to identify potential problems early. Common metrics include accuracy, response time, error rates, usage levels, and user satisfaction. Dashboards can provide a visual summary of these metrics over time, highlighting trends and anomalies. Alerts notify teams when metrics fall outside acceptable ranges. For example, if a translation app's accuracy drops below 85% or response time exceeds 5 seconds, an automatic alert can inform the technical team to investigate. Alerts can be threshold-based, trend-based, or comparative, depending on the type of issue being monitored.

Handling Failures and Quick Recovery

Monitoring is most useful when combined with well-defined procedures for handling failures. Reliable AI systems use graceful degradation, allowing the system to continue operating at reduced capacity when part of it fails. They also implement quick recovery strategies, such as rolling back to a previous version or using fallback algorithms, so users experience minimal disruption. A navigation app, for instance, might use real-time traffic routes under normal operation, fall back to historical traffic patterns if data fails, or provide basic map directions if the AI system is entirely unavailable.

Continuous Improvement

Monitoring systems support continuous improvement by providing feedback on AI performance. Regular updates—whether retraining models with new data, optimizing algorithms, or fixing identified issues—keep the AI accurate and efficient. Lessons learned from failures can inform preventive measures and system enhancements, ensuring that AI becomes more reliable over time.

7.6 Conclusion

As we wrap up our exploration of AI quality control and system reliability, it's clear that these practices form the foundation of trust between AI systems and the people who use them. Trust develops when users can predict how an AI system will behave, feel confident it will perform when needed, and know that problems will be handled effectively.

Reliable AI systems share several key characteristics: consistent performance, graceful handling of failures, continuous improvement based on feedback, and the presence of human oversight. Consistency lets users know what to expect, transparency helps them understand decision-making, responsive improvement ensures issues are addressed quickly, and human involvement maintains accountability and control. Together, these elements create an environment where AI can be trusted as a dependable partner in decision-making.

The principles we've covered in this chapter provide a practical framework for building and maintaining reliable AI. Start simple and gradually increase complexity, continuously monitor performance, plan for potential failures, and use every problem as an opportunity to improve the system. Keep humans involved throughout, ensuring they can understand, monitor, and override AI decisions when necessary.

For your future work in data analytics and AI applications, these skills and perspectives are essential. You should be able to measure basic AI performance, identify warning signs of failure, implement monitoring systems, and maintain accountability for decisions. By focusing on reliability, responsiveness, and user experience, you can contribute to AI systems that people not only use but trust. Building trust through reliable AI is not just a technical challenge—it's a professional responsibility and is a key to long-term success in the field.

Chapter 8

Designing Intelligent Business Systems

8.1 Introduction

Imagine walking into an office where your computer already knows what you need to work on today, your calendar has automatically rescheduled meetings based on urgent priorities, and routine reports have been generated and sent to the right people before you've even sat down. This isn't science fiction; it's the reality that many businesses are already creating intelligent systems.

You've probably experienced simple versions of this automation in your daily life. When Netflix suggests movies you might like, when your bank automatically categorizes your expenses, or when your email filters spam messages, you're interacting with intelligent business systems. These systems learn from data, make decisions, and take actions to make processes smoother and more efficient.

In our previous chapters, we've explored how AI systems work, make decisions, collaborate with humans, maintain quality, and operate ethically. Now we're ready to learn how to design complete intelligent business systems that can transform how organizations operate while working seamlessly with people.

The goal isn't to replace human workers but to create systems that handle routine tasks so people can focus on creative, strategic, and relationship-building work that humans do best. When designed thoughtfully, intelligent business systems can make work more interesting, reduce errors, and help organizations serve their customers better.

This chapter will teach you how to think like a system designer, identify the best opportunities for automation, and create intelligent systems that enhance human capabilities. You'll learn fundamental design principles, discover high-value automation opportunities, and understand how to balance automation with appropriate human oversight.

8.2 Principles for Designing Intelligent Systems

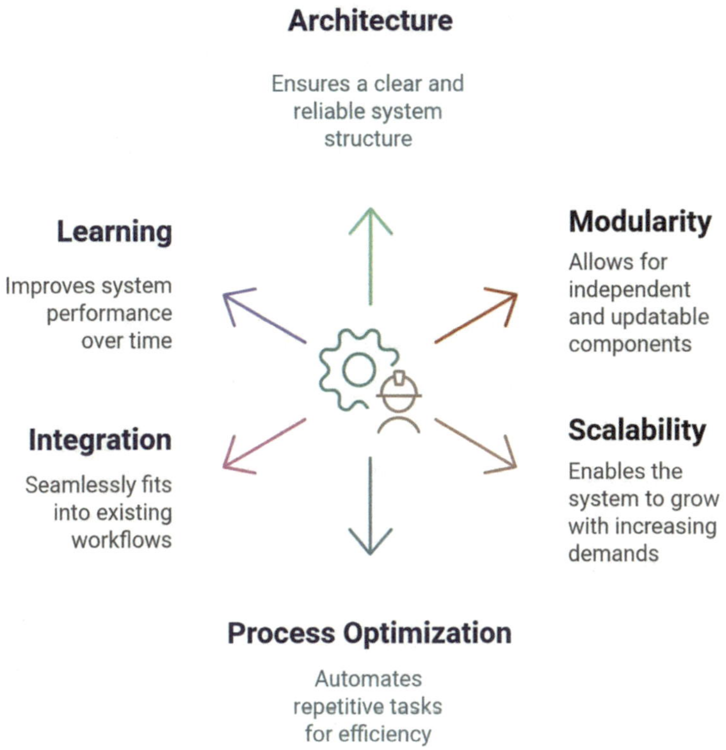

Understanding System Architecture Creating effective intelligent business systems requires understanding fundamental design principles that ensure these systems work reliably, integrate smoothly with existing processes, and deliver real value. At the heart of every intelligent system is its architecture, which functions like a blueprint for a building. It defines how different components connect and interact, and a well-designed architecture ensures the system is reliable, flexible, and scalable.

Modular Design One key principle is modular design. Modular systems are built from separate components that can operate independently while still connecting with other parts of the system. This approach allows organizations to update or improve one part without disrupting the rest of the system, making the system more flexible and easier to maintain. For example, an online store might have separate modules for customer service, product recommendations, and inventory management. The customer service module could handle chatbot conversations, the recommendation module could analyze customer behavior to suggest products, and the inventory module could track stock levels and predict demand. If the company wants to improve its chatbot, it can update the customer service module without affecting the recommendation or inventory modules, keeping the system stable and adaptable.

Scalability is another important principle. Intelligent systems should be able to handle growth, whether that means more users, more data, or more complex tasks, without slowing down or failing. Systems can scale horizontally, by adding more servers or computers, or vertically, by improving the performance of existing machines. Cloud-based architecture offers flexible scaling, automatically adjusting resources to meet demand. For instance, a bank's fraud detection system might start with a few servers handling a modest number of transactions per day, but as the bank grows, it can add servers, improve algorithms, and eventually use distributed cloud infrastructure to process millions of transactions daily. The modular design allows each component of the system to scale independently based on demand.

Process optimization through AI focuses on identifying repetitive, rule-based, and time-consuming tasks that can be automated. Not all tasks are suitable for automation; those requiring human judgment, creativity, or emotional intelligence should remain human-led. In a healthcare clinic, routine administrative tasks such as sending appointment reminders, verifying insurance coverage, processing lab results, and handling prescription refills can be automated, freeing up medical staff to focus on patient consultations, treatment planning, and emergency response. By targeting the right processes, AI can make workflows faster, more accurate, and less prone to error while supporting, rather than replacing, human decision-making.

Integration with existing workflows is critical for successful AI adoption. Intelligent systems should enhance current processes rather than disrupt them. A thoughtful approach involves starting with simple automations, maintaining familiar interfaces, allowing users to override AI decisions when necessary, and ensuring transparency so users understand what the AI is doing. For example, a marketing team might use AI tools to assist with audience research and generate initial content drafts while humans continue to lead brainstorming, refine the content, and make final decisions. This ensures that AI complements human work rather than replaces it, resulting in a smoother transition and greater user acceptance.

Finally, intelligent systems should be designed for continuous learning and adaptation. Self-improving systems gather data on performance, recognize patterns, adjust algorithms, and monitor whether changes enhance outcomes. Feedback loops are a key part of this process. An e-commerce chatbot, for instance, might start by answering only a portion of customer questions successfully, but over time it can learn from interactions, refine its responses, and adapt to seasonal patterns and changing promotions. Similarly, an inventory management system can adjust ordering patterns by learning from customer demand, sales performance, and supplier reliability. These continuous improvements allow intelligent systems to become more effective, efficient, and reliable without constant human intervention.

By applying these principles—modular design, scalability, process optimization, workflow integration, and continuous learning—organizations can design AI-driven systems that integrate smoothly with existing business processes and deliver meaningful improvements in efficiency and effectiveness.

8.3 High-Value Automation Opportunities

8.3.1 Recognizing Automation Candidates

Not all business processes are equally suited for automation. The most successful AI-driven systems focus on tasks that are repetitive, rule-based, and time-consuming, leaving creative, strategic, and relationship-oriented work to humans. Tasks that happen frequently, involve straightforward rules, or require managing large volumes of data are ideal candidates. In contrast, activities that demand judgment, complex problem-solving, or emotional intelligence should remain human-led.

For example, in an insurance claims process, routine document handling can be automated: incoming claims can be classified by type, key data extracted, suspicious cases flagged for review, and customers notified of progress automatically. Meanwhile, human adjusters focus on complex investigations, personalized customer communication, and final approvals. By targeting the right tasks, automation improves efficiency without sacrificing quality.

8.3.2 Evaluating Costs and Benefits

Before implementing automation, organizations must weigh the potential benefits against the required costs and effort. Benefits include time savings, fewer errors, consistent outcomes, the ability to scale processes, and improved employee satisfaction. Costs can include development time, software or hardware expenses, staff training, and ongoing maintenance.

Consider an accounting firm evaluating automated invoice processing. Manual data entry consumes five hours daily with a 2% error rate. By automating, the firm expects to reduce time spent by 80%, lower errors to 0.5%, and increase capacity threefold, allowing staff to focus on higher-value advisory work. The initial investment pays for itself within a few months, demonstrating a clear business case.

8.3.3 Automated Reporting and Decision Support

Automation can also enhance reporting and decision-making workflows. AI systems can gather and analyze data from multiple sources to produce timely, consistent reports, such as daily sales summaries, inventory updates, or compliance documentation. By freeing managers from routine analysis, these systems allow staff to focus on interpreting insights and making strategic decisions.

Decision support systems extend this concept by providing recommendations rather than taking final action. For instance, a hospital staffing system might analyze patient census data, staff schedules, and historical trends to forecast demand and recommend staffing levels. Human managers retain final authority, handling exceptions, ensuring policy compliance, and verifying quality standards. This combination of AI analytics and human judgment ensures both efficiency and accountability.

8.3.4 Predictive Analytics Applications

Predictive analytics leverages historical data and AI to anticipate future events, enabling proactive decision-making. In manufacturing, predictive maintenance systems use sensor data to forecast equipment failures, schedule repairs at convenient times, and reduce costly downtime. Similarly, in e-commerce, predictive analytics can anticipate customer purchases, optimize inventory, and forecast support needs, improving service while streamlining operations.

For example, an online retailer can analyze browsing patterns, past purchases, and seasonal trends to predict when customers are likely to buy specific products. Automated recommendations and proactive inventory adjustments help the company serve customers efficiently and reduce waste or stockouts.

8.3.5 Implementing Automation Successfully

Effective automation requires careful planning, stakeholder engagement, and attention to change management. Introducing AI often changes established workflows, so employees need clear communication about the purpose and benefits of automation, hands-on training, and opportunities to provide feedback. Gradual implementation through pilot programs allows staff to adapt without disruption.

A bank implementing automated loan processing, for instance, started with volunteer officers to test the system, collected feedback to refine workflows, provided comprehensive training, and maintained a support network of experienced users. After six months, 95% of employees reported satisfaction, and loan processing time dropped by 60%.

8.3.6 Measuring Success

Finally, organizations must track automation performance through clear metrics. Key measures include efficiency gains, error reduction, cost savings, customer satisfaction, and employee engagement. For example, a telecommunications company tracking its customer service chatbot measures average response time, resolution rate, customer satisfaction, and business impact, including cost per interaction and agent productivity. These metrics help identify whether the automation is delivering expected value and highlight areas for continuous improvement.

By systematically identifying automation candidates, evaluating costs and benefits, leveraging predictive and decision-support systems, implementing change management, and measuring outcomes, organizations can focus their AI efforts on high-value opportunities. This ensures that intelligent systems deliver meaningful improvements while maintaining human oversight where it is most critical.

8.4 Balancing Automation and Human Oversight

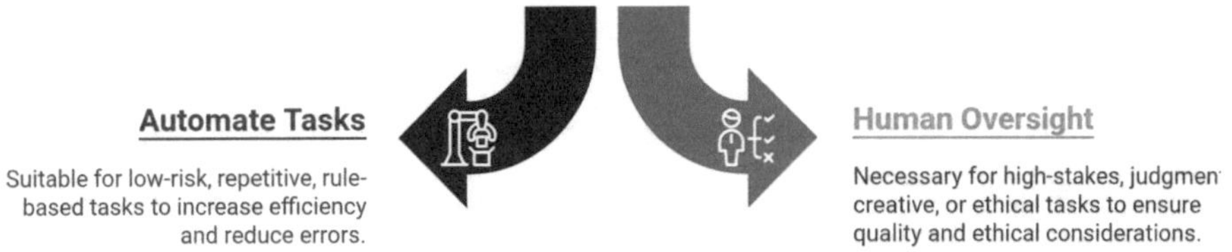

Determining Automation Boundaries

Not every task should be fully automated. Understanding where to draw the line between automated processes and human oversight is essential for building systems that are both efficient and trustworthy. Tasks that are predictable, rule-based, and low-risk are ideal for full automation, while activities that involve judgment, emotional intelligence, or high stakes require human involvement.

Tasks Suitable for Full Automation

Full automation works best for repetitive, rule-driven, and data-driven tasks with well-defined inputs and outputs. These processes are predictable, time-sensitive, and carry low risk if errors occur.

For instance, in online banking, tasks like account balance inquiries, automatic bill payments, and fraud alerts can be fully automated. Retrieving a customer's balance or processing scheduled payments involves clear rules and predictable data, making automation reliable. Similarly, AI can detect unusual transaction patterns and send alerts, where occasional false positives are easily corrected and do not pose serious risk.

Tasks Requiring Human Judgment

Certain tasks demand human oversight due to their complexity, ethical considerations, or potential consequences. Human involvement is critical for decisions that require emotional intelligence, creative problem-solving, or high-stakes judgment.

In healthcare, AI can assist with medical diagnosis, treatment planning, and patient communication, but doctors and nurses maintain control. AI may analyze symptoms or suggest treatment options, but human professionals review recommendations, consider patient-specific factors, and provide empathy and explanation. This combination ensures patient safety, ethical care, and high-quality outcomes.

Designing Human-AI Collaboration

Effective systems leverage the complementary strengths of humans and AI. Humans excel at creativity, ethical reasoning, contextual understanding, and adaptability, while AI is unmatched in processing large datasets, identifying patterns, maintaining consistency, and performing routine tasks quickly.

For example, a law firm can combine AI and human expertise in legal research. AI scans thousands of documents, identifies relevant precedents, and highlights trends, while lawyers interpret findings, develop strategy, consult with clients, and present arguments in court. By clearly defining responsibilities, the system enables higher efficiency and better outcomes without sacrificing human judgment.

Escalation and Override Mechanisms

Well-designed systems provide clear rules for when humans should intervene in automated processes. Escalation can be triggered by low AI confidence, exceptions outside normal parameters, high-risk situations, customer requests, or regulatory requirements.

An e-commerce company's chatbot illustrates this approach: if the AI's confidence in a response falls below a set threshold or a customer expresses distress, the conversation is escalated to a human agent. The handoff includes complete context, ensuring continuity. Human agents, managers, and even customers retain override capabilities, ensuring accountability and control.

Accountability and Transparency

Maintaining accountability and transparency is critical when humans and AI collaborate. Decision audit trails record input data, AI analyses, human reviews, final decisions, and outcomes, enabling oversight, compliance, and continuous improvement.

A bank's AI-assisted loan approval process, for example, documents every step, from data collection and risk assessment to human review and final decision, supporting regulatory compliance, quality assurance, and dispute resolution.

Explainable AI for Informed Oversight

Explainable AI helps humans understand how automated systems arrive at their recommendations. Different levels of explanation—from simple summaries for users to detailed analyses for experts—build trust and support informed decision-making.

In medical diagnostics, an AI might provide patients with a clear summary of suggested conditions and key supporting factors, while doctors receive detailed analyses including symptom contributions, test interpretations, literature references, and confidence levels. This allows professionals to make well-informed, accountable decisions.

Building Trust in Automated Systems

Trust is essential for effective human-AI collaboration. Users need clarity on system capabilities, limitations, and control options. Transparent communication about accuracy, potential risks, and when human oversight is required fosters confidence.

For example, a financial advisory AI explicitly communicates what it can and cannot do, provides performance metrics, and allows clients to accept, modify, or reject recommendations. Human advisors remain available for consultation, ensuring that users retain ultimate control and responsibility.

By carefully defining automation boundaries, leveraging complementary strengths, implementing escalation mechanisms, maintaining accountability, and providing explainable AI, organizations can balance efficiency with oversight. This approach ensures intelligent systems are reliable, ethical, and trustworthy while keeping humans in control of critical decisions.

8.5 Conclusion

As we conclude our exploration of designing intelligent business systems, the goal is not to replace human workers, but to create technology that enhances their work, making it more meaningful, efficient, and impactful. Intelligent systems are most effective when designed with people at the center, understanding both the tasks that can be automated and the work that benefits from human judgment, creativity, and empathy.

In designing intelligent business systems, the aim is to enhance—not replace—human work, making it more meaningful and efficient.

Successful systems begin by identifying tasks that are repetitive, rule-based, and data-driven, automating these processes to save time and reduce errors. At the same time, tasks that require complex decision-making, emotional intelligence, or ethical judgment remain under human oversight. By carefully balancing automation with human control, organizations can ensure reliability, accountability, and better overall outcomes.

Designing effective intelligent systems relies on several fundamental principles. Modular and scalable architecture allows systems to adapt and grow without disrupting existing workflows. Continuous learning and feedback loops ensure that systems improve over time, becoming more effective while maintaining alignment with human needs. Integration with current processes, combined with transparency and explainable AI, builds trust and enables users to understand, interact with, and guide automated systems confidently.

Ultimately, the most successful intelligent business systems do more than increase efficiency—they empower people to focus on creative problem-solving, strategic thinking, relationship building, and high-stakes decision-making. By combining automation with thoughtful human oversight, organizations can create systems that not only perform reliably but also enhance human capabilities and workplace satisfaction.

Made in the USA
Monee, IL
05 November 2026

67857687R00072